DATE DUE

OC 08 07			
GAYLORD			PRINTED IN U.S.A.

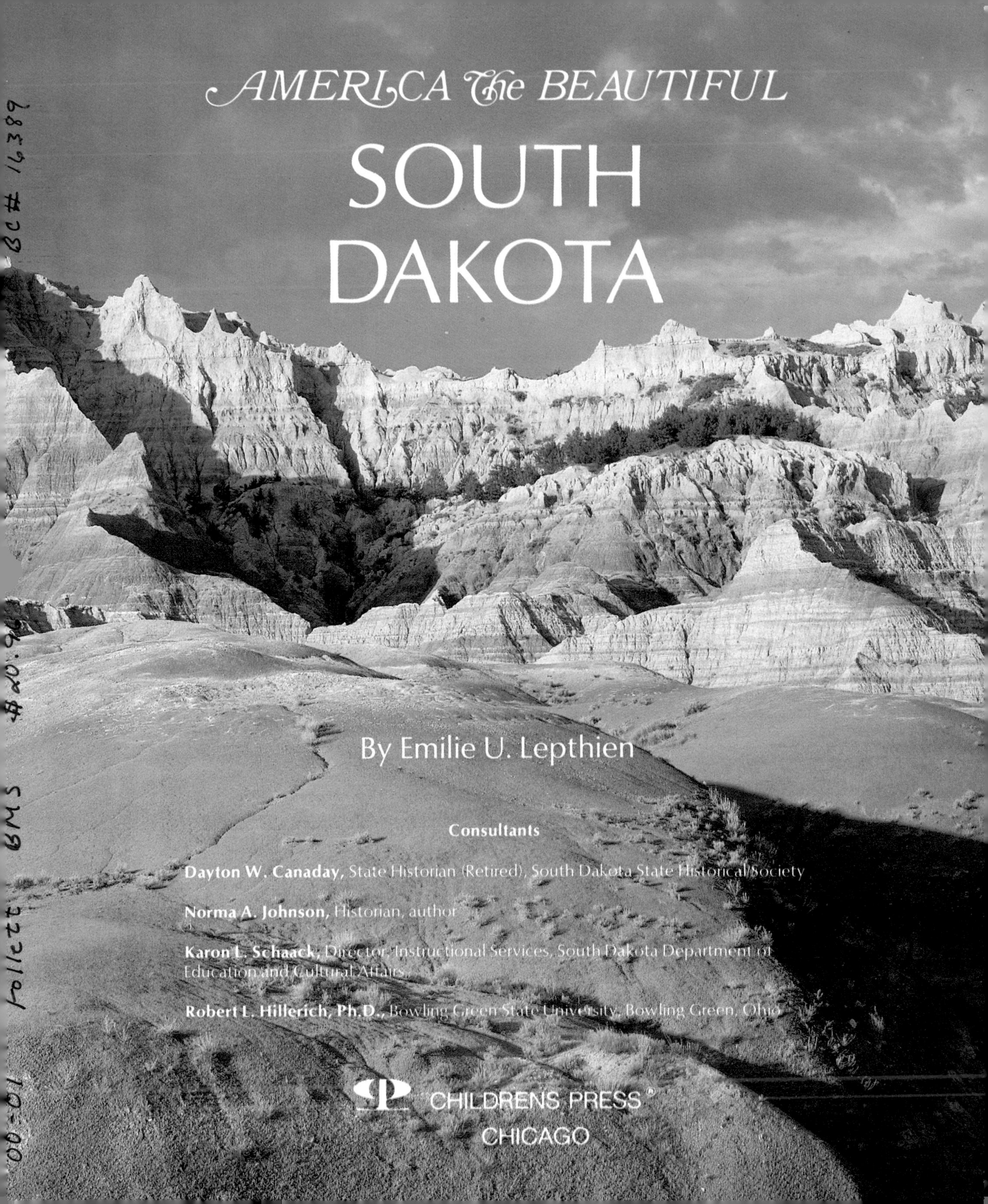

AMERICA the BEAUTIFUL
SOUTH
DAKOTA

By Emilie U. Lepthien

Consultants

Dayton W. Canaday, State Historian (Retired), South Dakota State Historical Society

Norma A. Johnson, Historian, author

Karon L. Schaack, Director, Instructional Services, South Dakota Department of Education and Cultural Affairs

Robert L. Hillerich, Ph.D., Bowling Green State University, Bowling Green, Ohio

CHILDRENS PRESS®
CHICAGO

Two young residents of eastern South Dakota

Project Editor: Joan Downing
Associate Editor: Shari Joffe
Design Director: Margrit Fiddle
Typesetting: Graphic Connections, Inc.
Engraving: Liberty Photoengraving

Library of Congress Cataloging-in-Publication Data

Lepthien, Emilie U. (Emilie Utteg)
    America the beautiful. South Dakota / by Emilie U.
Lepthien.
        p.   cm.
    Includes index.
    Summary: Introduces the geography, history,
government, economy, industry, culture, historic
sites, and famous people of the state nicknamed the
"Land of Infinite Variety."
    ISBN 0-516-00487-5
    1. South Dakota—Juvenile literature. [1. South
Dakota] I. Title.
F636.3.L47   1991   90-21137
978.3—dc20   CIP
                                                     AC

Silos on a South Dakota farm

TABLE OF CONTENTS

Chapter 1 Land of Infinite Variety 7

Chapter 2 The Land 9

Chapter 3 The People 21

Chapter 4 Beginnings 27

Chapter 5 Pioneer Days 37

Chapter 6 The Centennial Years 51

Chapter 7 Government and the Economy 61

Chapter 8 Culture and Recreation 73

Chapter 9 Touring the Sunshine State 87

Facts at a Glance 109

Maps 133

Index 138

Chapter 1
LAND OF
INFINITE VARIETY

LAND OF INFINITE VARIETY

From fertile fields and rolling hills in the east, to parched rock formations in the western Badlands, to pine forests and granite peaks in the southwestern Black Hills, South Dakota's landscape paints a picture of infinite variety. In fact, Land of Infinite Variety is one of South Dakota's nicknames. Along with this variety of geographic features come varying weather conditions—from droughts in the summer to blizzards in the winter. Even so, South Dakota's official nickname is the Sunshine State. Hardly a day goes by without the sun shining brightly on the state.

Many groups of people have inhabited the land that became South Dakota—from prehistoric peoples to the present-day Sioux, or Dakota, Indians, for whom the state was named. In the late 1800s, as covered wagons and railroads pushed the edge of civilization westward, the region experienced its first modern development. Transportation brought settlers—farmers, ranchers, miners, storekeepers, land agents, physicians, printers—all desiring free land in the "new frontier."

Some of South Dakota's most famous residents, including Sitting Bull, Wild Bill Hickok, and Laura Ingalls Wilder, lived during those frontier days. In more recent years, South Dakotans have been able to point with pride to Hubert H. Humphrey and George S. McGovern, native sons who became Democratic candidates for president of the United States. Since 1980, South Dakota's expanding industries have attracted thousands of new residents. In addition, millions of tourists each year enjoy the Sunshine State's infinite variety of natural, historic, and man-made attractions.

Chapter 2

THE LAND

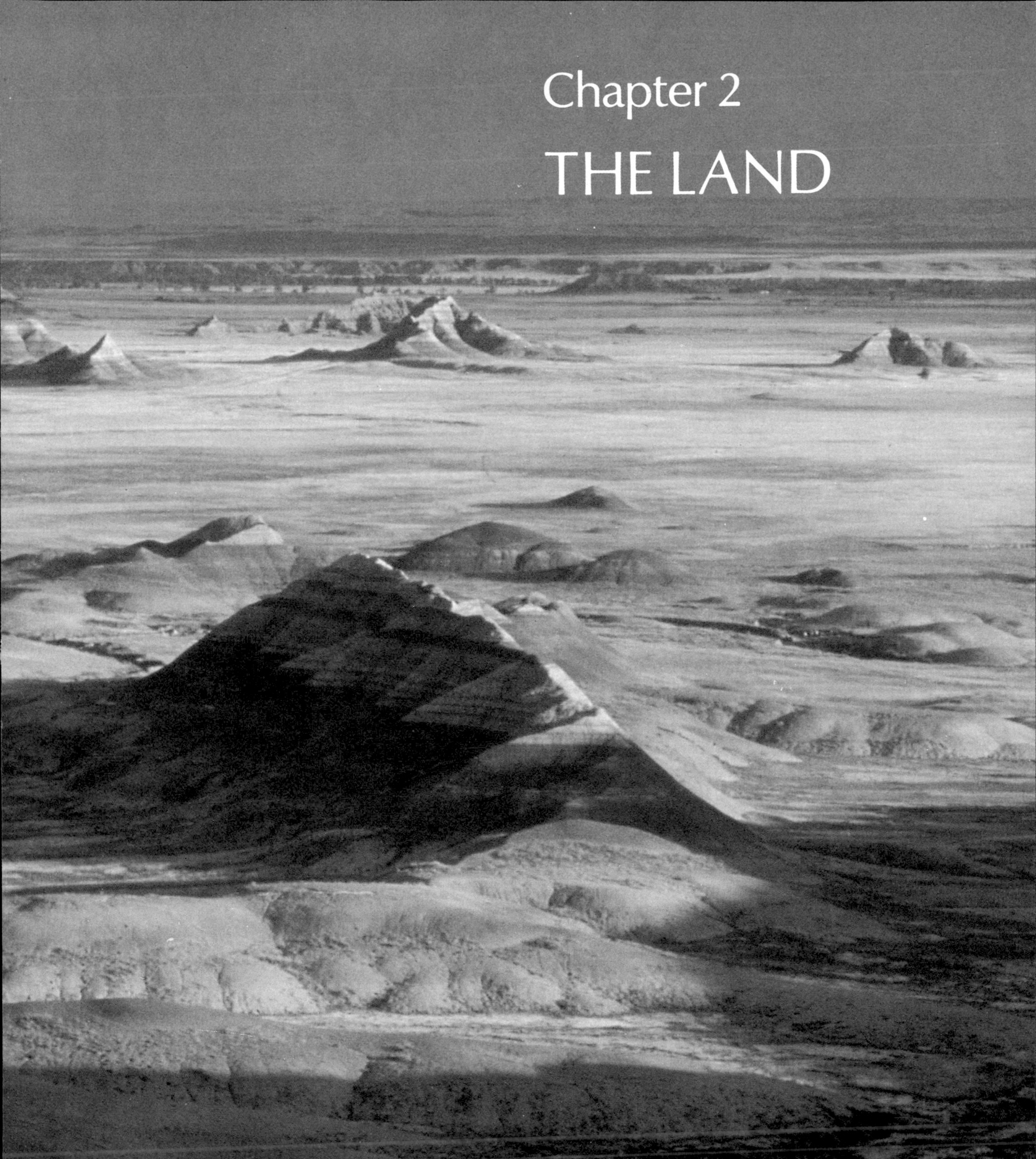

THE LAND

GEOGRAPHY AND TOPOGRAPHY

South Dakota ranks sixteenth in area among the United States.
Its 77,116 square miles (199,730 square kilometers) are bordered
by North Dakota on the north, Minnesota and Iowa on the east,
Nebraska on the south, and Montana and Wyoming on the west.

The geographical center of the state is in Hughes County,
8 miles (13 kilometers) northeast of Pierre (pronounced ''peer''),
the state capital. The geographical center of the United States is
17 miles (27 kilometers) west of Castle Rock, near South Dakota's
western boundary.

Flowing southward through the entire state, the Missouri River
nearly cuts South Dakota in half, dividing it into two very
different land regions. South Dakotans use the terms *East River*
and *West River* to describe the differences between both the land
and the people on each side of the river. South Dakota's three land
regions are the East River Prairie Plains, the West River Great
Plains, and the Black Hills.

THE PRAIRIE PLAINS

During the Ice Age, the Missouri River formed the western
boundary of the glaciers that moved south across the north-
central part of the United States. East of the Missouri, the glaciers

South Dakota's Prairie Plains region is one of the most profitable agricultural areas in the nation.

scraped and gouged the land, leveling off the higher places, filling in the valleys, and creating lakes and marshes.

Today, most of this East River Country is called the Prairie Plains. This area is made up of two regions: the Drift Prairie and the Dissected Till Plains. The Drift Prairie, which covers most of the eastern third of the state, features low, rolling hills and about 120 glacial lakes. The gently rolling hills of the Dissected Till Plains extend over South Dakota's southeastern corner. The land of the Prairie Plains provides fertile soil for growing spring wheat, oats, and corn, and for grazing sheep, dairy cattle, and beef cattle. This region is one of the most profitable agricultural areas in the United States.

The state's lowest point, Big Stone Lake, lies on the northeastern edge of this region. Most of the other lakes of the Prairie Plains are also located in the northeast.

South Dakota's famed Badlands lie in the southwestern part of the state.

THE GREAT PLAINS

Most of the western two-thirds of South Dakota is covered by the Great Plains. The part of the Great Plains east of the Missouri River and extending almost to the James River is marked with glacial hills and canyonlike valleys. West of the Missouri, canyons and buttes add variety to expanses of flat, level plains. Buttes are steep, flat-topped hills that, in South Dakota, rise up to 600 feet (183 meters) above the plains. The most striking of South Dakota's buttes jut up in the northeastern part of the state.

In the southwestern section of the Great Plains, the Badlands—one of South Dakota's most spectacular features—extend for over 100 miles (161 kilometers) between the White and Cheyenne rivers. The Indians called the area *mako* (land) *sica* (bad), and French explorers referred to it as *les mauvaises terres a traverser,*

South Dakota's Great Plains region includes both plains (left) and the rugged, colorful Badlands (right).

"the bad lands to travel across." More than a hundred years later, Lieutenant Colonel George Custer described them as "a part of Hell with the fires burned out." On the northern rim, an 80-mile- (129-kilometer-) long wall marks a steep drop-off from the flat, grassy prairie to the rugged, eroded land below.

Over millions of years, wind and water erosion have shaped the soft sandstone and clay of the Badlands into peaks, spires, cliffs, and gullies of varying colors. Purple hues come from oxidized manganese; orange and tan, from oxidized iron; white, from volcanic ash; and gray, from silt and clay. Although there is little plant or animal life in the region today, saber-toothed tigers, rhinoceroses, three-toed horses, and small camels lived there over 25 million years ago. After a heavy rain, geologists and tourists can still find fossils of these creatures.

Roughlock Falls in the Black Hills National Forest

Although the Great Plains region has little tillable soil for
growing crops, it contains 22 million acres (9 million hectares) of
grazing land. Large buffalo herds that once roamed the Great
Plains grazed on a native grass now known as buffalo grass.
Today, vast areas of buffalo grass are protected in the Fort Pierre,
Grand River, and Buffalo Gap national grasslands.

THE BLACK HILLS

In sharp contrast to the Great Plains, the Black Hills rise up
suddenly at the southwestern edge of the state. From a distance,
the dark-green, densely forested hills appear black. The hills are
sacred to the Sioux, who named them *Pahá Sápa*, meaning "hills
that are black."

These hills are actually domed mountains formed long before

the Rockies, Alps, or Himalayas. The Black Hills contain South Dakota's highest point. Rising 7,242 feet (2,207 meters) above sea level, Harney Peak is also the highest peak east of the Rockies.

Beneath the Black Hills lie rich veins of gold and other minerals, such as silver and mica. Most of the state's forestland lies within the region. Rapid City, South Dakota's second-largest city, flourishes on the eastern edge of the Black Hills.

The Mammoth Site, located in the southeastern corner of the Black Hills, is one of the state's treasure troves of prehistoric animal remains. In 1974, workers bulldozing for a housing project uncovered several mammoth bones. Since then, tusks, teeth, and bones of at least forty-one mammoths have been uncovered there.

RIVERS AND LAKES

The Missouri River, whose headwaters are in Montana, flows for 547 miles (880 kilometers) through South Dakota. All of the state's rivers flow into the Missouri, except for those in the northeast corner, which drain into Big Stone Lake and Lake Traverse.

In East River Country, the Big Sioux, Vermillion, and James rivers flow south to reach the Missouri. In the city of Sioux Falls, the Big Sioux River drops 20 feet (6 meters) in a series of spectacular waterfalls. In West River Country, the Grand, Moreau, Belle Fourche, Cheyenne, Bad, and White rivers flow east to join the Missouri.

The retreating glaciers formed most of the state's northeastern lakes. Medicine Lake, in central Codington County, has an unusual attribute for an inland lake: it has a higher salt content than sea water. Big Stone and Waubay lakes, and Lakes Traverse, Poinsett, and Thompson, are among the state's largest natural lakes. Between 1946 and 1966, Lewis and Clark Lake and Lakes Oahe, Francis Case, and Sharpe were formed by building four dams on the Missouri River. Known as the Great Lakes of South Dakota, these are the state's four largest lakes.

CLIMATE

Although South Dakota is known as the Sunshine State, some people think of it as the Blizzard State. These two contrasting nicknames are evidence of the extremes in the state's weather conditions. Summer temperatures often climb to over 100 degrees Fahrenheit (38 degrees Celsius), and winter temperatures can dip far below freezing. South Dakota's highest recorded temperature, 120 degrees Fahrenheit (49 degrees Celsius), occurred at Gann Valley on July 5, 1936. The state's record low of minus 58 degrees Fahrenheit (minus 50 degrees Celsius) occurred at McIntosh on February 17, 1936.

Temperatures and precipitation also vary from one part of the state to another. In the south-central part of the state, the average July temperature is 78 degrees Fahrenheit (26 degrees Celsius). In the Black Hills, the July average is 68 degrees Fahrenheit (20 degrees Celsius). Throughout South Dakota, summer days are usually pleasant; the state is known for its relatively low humidity. In the northeast, the average January temperature is 10 degrees Fahrenheit (minus 12 degrees Celsius), while in the Black Hills, it is 24 degrees Fahrenheit (minus 4 degrees Celsius).

Annual precipitation (rainfall and melted snow) averages about 13 inches (33 centimeters) in the northwest and about 25 inches (64 centimeters) in the southeast. Because of its higher altitude, the Black Hills region receives more precipitation than the rest of western South Dakota. Snowfall in South Dakota averages from

A winter scene near the Missouri River in central South Dakota

22 to 60 inches (56 to 152 centimeters) a year, with as much as
100 inches (254 centimeters) in the Black Hills.

South Dakota's famous blizzards—snowstorms with winds
reaching 70 miles (113 kilometers) per hour—can be so violent
that parts of the West River area are buried under snow for weeks.
Livestock become stranded on the range, and the United States Air
Force and private pilots drop food to them through "haylifts."

Too little snow, however, means not enough moisture for
spring crops. This, combined with little or no summer rain, can
lead to drought conditions. The crops wither and die in the fields,
and the soil turns to dust, blowing away in dust storms. Only the
hardiest of people can withstand the challenges of South Dakota's
weather from year to year.

ANIMAL AND PLANT LIFE

South Dakota is sometimes called the Coyote State because coyotes roam the open prairies and plains. Although they are a threat to sheep, they also help control the jackrabbit population.

At one time, millions of buffalo roamed over South Dakota's Great Plains. By the 1880s, these animals were nearly extinct because hunters had killed so many of them for sport as well as for meat and hides. Today, the state has about eight thousand buffalo—more than any other state. Protected herds of buffalo live in Custer State Park and Wind Cave National Park in the Black Hills. Buffalo are also raised on private ranches.

The Black Hills are also home to bighorn sheep, elk, Rocky Mountain goats, and a large number of the state's white-tailed deer. Pronghorn antelope and mule deer inhabit the plains west of the Missouri River. Beavers, muskrats, foxes, bobcats, skunks, raccoons, opossums, porcupines, and prairie dogs are found throughout the state. Rattlesnakes pose a danger in the west.

South Dakota's grasslands, prairies, waterways, mountains, and forests provide a home, at least part of the year, to more than three hundred species of birds. Bald and golden eagles can be sighted in the Badlands and in the southern Missouri Valley. Ducks and Canada geese migrate south along the Missouri each fall. Rare trumpeter swans nest in and near La Creek National Wildlife Refuge. Hungarian partridges, sage grouse, sharp-tailed grouse, wild turkeys, and Chinese ring-necked pheasants (the state bird) make South Dakota a hunter's paradise.

The state's lakes and rivers are filled with fish. Bass, bluegills, crappies, perch, and walleyed and northern pike abound in the glacial lakes of the northeast. Catfish, walleyed and northern pike, Chinook salmon, paddlefish, sauger, and sturgeon are plentiful in

South Dakota's colorful wildlife includes such birds as sharp-tailed grouse (above) and such wildflowers as larkspurs (right).

the Missouri River and its many tributaries. The lakes and streams of the Black Hills yield brook, brown, and rainbow trout.

Forests cover less than 4 percent of the state. Pines, junipers, and spruces grow in the Black Hills and Custer national forests. Ashes, aspens, cottonwoods, elms, oaks, and willows occur sparsely—mostly along rivers—throughout the rest of the state.

The lavender pasqueflower, South Dakota's state flower, blossoms on sunny hillsides in the springtime. Wild orange geraniums, black-eyed Susans, mariposa lilies, roses, and poppies form a carpet of color on the prairies in the central part of the state. In the Black Hills, bluebells, forget-me-nots, lady's-slippers, and larkspurs bloom. Pink- and yellow-flowered cactus plants are found close to the ground in western South Dakota.

19

Chapter 3
THE PEOPLE

THE PEOPLE

POPULATION AND POPULATION DISTRIBUTION

The 1990 census counted 696,004 South Dakotans, a gain of about 1 percent over the 1980 census. Among the fifty states, South Dakota ranks forty-fifth in population.

South Dakota is one of the few states that has more people living in rural areas than in urban areas. About 30 percent of the population reside in metropolitan areas, while about 70 percent live on farms or ranches or in small towns.

The state's overall population density is 9 persons per square mile (3.5 persons per square kilometer). In West River Country, however, there are only about 2 persons per square mile (0.7 persons per square kilometer). Indian reservations, national grasslands, and range for cattle ranching cover much of the land in this region.

South Dakota has only ten cities with more than ten thousand people: Sioux Falls, Rapid City, Aberdeen, Watertown, Brookings, Mitchell, Pierre, Yankton, Huron, and Vermillion. Except for Rapid City, all of these cities are located east of the Missouri River. Most of them grew along the banks of the Big Sioux, James, or Vermillion rivers on the fertile Prairie Plains. The two largest cities are located on interstate highways. These cities provide services to the many farm families who live in East River Country.

Sioux Falls, in the southeastern part of the state, is South Dakota's largest city.

Rapid City and several other towns and cities in the Black Hills, including Custer, Spearfish, Sturgis, Hot Springs, Lead, and Deadwood, have developed because of the mining, forestry, and tourism industries.

WHO ARE THE SOUTH DAKOTANS?

In the early 1800s, American Indians (Native Americans) of the Sioux Federation's seven tribes, forced out of Minnesota by the Chippewa, began arriving in present-day South Dakota. Four of these seven tribes—the Mdewakanton, Wakpekute, Wahpeton, and Sisseton—were known collectively as the Santee. They spoke the Dakota version of the Sioux language. Most of the Santee eventually settled in Minnesota. The Yankton and Yanktonai Sioux, who spoke the Nakota language, settled in the eastern part of the Dakota region. The largest of the seven Sioux tribes, the Teton Sioux, settled in the West River Country. The Teton Sioux spoke the Lakota language and were composed of seven subtribes.

Most of the Sioux who remain in South Dakota today belong to the Sisseton, Yankton, Yanktonai, and Teton tribes. Of the seven Teton subtribes, the best known in South Dakota's history have been the Brûlé, Oglala, and Hunkpapa. Today, most of the Sioux live on or near the state's eight Indian reservations. Many move back and forth between their reservation and such cities as Rapid City, Pierre, Sioux Falls, and Yankton.

Among South Dakota's first white settlers were farmers from Wisconsin, Minnesota, and Iowa. Many of them had originally come from New England, New York, and Pennsylvania. Thousands of immigrants from Norway, Sweden, Denmark, Germany, Russia, Czechoslovakia, Hungary, Holland, Ireland, Scotland, Finland, and Poland established tightly knit communities, many of which still exist today. Most of these people settled in the eastern part of the state. By 1890, one-third of the white residents of South Dakota were foreign born. In the 1870s and 1880s, a few hundred Chinese came from California and set up businesses in Deadwood or worked in the nearby gold mines.

Today, more than 99 percent of South Dakota's residents were born in the United States, and 72 percent were born in South Dakota. German influence remains strong, however; 10 percent of the state's residents still claim German as their mother tongue. Nearly 92 percent of the state's population is white. South Dakota's fifty-one thousand Native Americans form the largest group of nonwhites, making up 7 percent of the state's population. Hispanics, African Americans, and Asians, most of whom arrived in the state after World War II, make up less than 1 percent of the population.

Statistics confirm that South Dakotans are law-abiding, independent, and hardworking. South Dakota has the third-

The influence of people of Scandinavian heritage on the state is reflected in the Chapel in the Hills near Rapid City, a replica of a famous 800-year-old Norwegian church.

lowest crime rate (after West Virginia and North Dakota) in the nation. South Dakota's farmers and business owners have helped the state claim the highest percentage of self-employed people in the United States. Although unemployment among the Native American population is between 60 and 80 percent, the unemployment rate for the population as a whole is a low 3.9 percent. Poor health and education, alcoholism, little job training, lack of economic development on the reservations, and discrimination contribute to the high Indian unemployment rate.

POLITICS

South Dakota has an almost equal number of registered Democrats and registered Republicans. However, throughout most of the state's history, voters have strongly favored Republican candidates for national and state offices. South Dakotans have given the majority of their votes to Democratic presidential candidates only four times: in 1896, to William McKinley; in 1932 and 1936, to Franklin D. Roosevelt; and in 1964, to Lyndon Johnson. Even when Democratic native sons Hubert H. Humphrey and George S. McGovern ran for the presidency (in 1968 and 1972 respectively), the majority of South Dakotans voted Republican.

Since 1889, Democrats have controlled the governorship for only eighteen years. Eight of these years were during the 1970s, when Democrats won the office three times and controlled most other state offices. Since 1979, most state offices have again been in the hands of the Republicans.

RELIGION

Early immigrants formed most of the state's churches. German-Russians, who fled religious persecution in Europe, established Mennonite and Hutterite Brethren churches in the James River valley. Today, fifty Hutterite colonies follow early Christian teachings of holding land and goods in common.

Lutherans make up the single-largest church group in South Dakota. Other Protestant groups include Methodists, Presbyterians, Episcopalians, Baptists, Mormons, and members of the United Church of Christ. Roman Catholics are the second-largest religious group in the state. The state's Jewish population numbers less than a thousand.

Some of the Sioux continue to practice their native religious beliefs in the Native American (Peyote) church. Most, however, belong to one of the many Christian denominations.

Chapter 4
BEGINNINGS

BEGINNINGS

Located midway between the Atlantic and Pacific oceans and the North Pole and the equator, the land of present-day South Dakota provided a migration route for many groups of ancient peoples. Descendants of people who crossed the Bering Strait, a land bridge between Asia and North America, migrated to the Dakota area more than ten thousand years ago. Much later, ancestors of present-day Plains Indians, including the Sioux, entered the land from the east and south.

THE FIRST SOUTH DAKOTANS

South of the Black Hills, at a campsite dating to 8000 B.C., archaeologists have found the earliest evidence of human life in the Dakota area. Other such sites, most of them in the Black Hills or along the Missouri River, have also been uncovered. Artifacts show that these people hunted for food and knew little about agriculture. Ice Age mammals, such as giant bisons, sloths, mammoths, and four-horned antelopes, provided the mainstay of the early people's diet. By about 5000 B.C., the climate had become hot and dry, causing these animals to die off. Adapting to this change, the people fished, hunted the smaller buffalo, and foraged for roots and berries.

Around A.D. 500, people known as Mound Builders began settling east of the Missouri River, mainly along the Big Sioux

River and on Big Stone Lake. There they built more than a hundred dome-shaped, earthen mounds that were used as burial chambers. Thirty-eight mounds once stood near Brandon. From the tools and weapons found in the mounds, archaeologists can tell that the Mound Builders hunted for their food. They made some of their tools out of hammered metal, and made simple line drawings on their pottery. About A.D. 800, the Mound Builders vanished, for no known reason. Some scholars theorize that they were wiped out by a disease epidemic.

AGRICULTURAL TRIBES

A few hundred years later, another Indian group built a fortified village of seventy lodges on the shore of Firesteel Creek. Archaeologists believe that about a thousand people lived there as farmers and hunters. Between 1250 and 1400, people believed to be ancestors of the Mandans left southern Minnesota and settled in farming villages along the rich bottomlands of the Missouri River. They built earth lodges, and, for many years, lived there in peace.

By 1325, some ten thousand people lived in about ten villages high on the bluffs above the Missouri River, all within 60 miles (97 kilometers) of the present-day Crow Creek Indian Reservation. Excavations at a site overlooking present-day Lake Francis Case have uncovered the remains of a fortified farming village dating from this time.

Sometime during the 1500s, a group known as the Arikara moved along the Missouri River from the Kansas-Nebraska region into present-day South Dakota. From present-day Yankton to the mouth of the Cheyenne River, they, too, established well-fortified farming villages on the bluffs along the Missouri River. Known as

The buffalo hunt, depicted here in a nineteenth-century painting by George Catlin, was an important part of Sioux life.

"corn-eaters" by neighboring tribes, the Arikara raised large crops of corn, as well as beans, pumpkins, squash, and tobacco. Buffalo hunting added meat to their diet. At trading fairs in the Black Hills, homeland of the Cheyenne tribe, the Arikara traded their surplus crops for horses, thus introducing these animals to the northern plains. The Arikara flourished until the mid-1700s, when disease and warfare began to take their toll and they began losing their territory to the migrating Sioux. By 1795, the Arikara had been pushed north to the mouth of the Grand River. Today, the Arikara live on or near the Fort Berthold Indian Reservation in North Dakota.

THE SIOUX

By 1750, the Ojibwa, or Chippewa, had forced most of the seven tribes of the Sioux Federation, including their subtribes, from what is now Minnesota into present-day South Dakota. Receiving guns from French traders had enabled the Chippewa to overpower the fierce Sioux. Named *Sioux* (meaning "enemy" or "snake") by the Chippewa, the Sioux called themselves the *Dakota*, which means "allies" or "friends." Through early French explorers, the Dakota became known as the Sioux to all white traders and explorers. The new land that the Dakota entered was later named after them.

Leaving the forests and lakes of the Minnesota area for the prairies and plains of Dakota brought changes to the Sioux way of life. The lightweight, skin-covered tepee, used for only part of the year in Minnesota, now became their only home. They no longer needed boats to transport themselves and their belongings. Instead, they used an apparatus called a travois (a net attached to two poles), which was pulled at first by dogs and then later by horses received in trade with the Arikara. On horseback, using their skill with the bow and arrow, the Sioux became great buffalo hunters and fierce warriors on the Great Plains. Buffalo meat replaced their diet of wild rice, berries, and small forest animals.

Sioux culture became centered on the buffalo hunt. A successful hunt provided everything the Sioux needed for a good life. Buffalo meat served as food; hides provided warm bedding, clothing, moccasins, and tepee coverings; sinew became sewing thread and string for their bows; bones and horns were worked into needles, spoons, and tools; and buffalo skulls were used in religious ceremonies. Extra meat and hides were traded for vegetables, horses, and other goods at trading fairs in the Black Hills and north on the James River.

The Sioux had a well-developed moral code based on the virtues of bravery, generosity, honor, and endurance. Selfishness was considered evil. They also believed that humans should live in harmony with nature and that the land could be owned by no

The Sioux used a device called a travois to transport their belongings
across the plains and prairies of Dakota.

one. Sioux society centered on the extended family, in which all
generations lived together, were respected, and had special work
to do. Everything was owned in common by the Sioux, except for
a person's horse. By 1780, the Sioux empire stretched across the
Great Plains from what is now Kansas, Nebraska, North Dakota,
and South Dakota to the Rocky Mountains. They had claimed the
Black Hills as sacred and holy ground.

EUROPEAN EXPLORERS AND TRADERS

During the same years that the Sioux spread across Dakota,
French explorers following the Minnesota River from the east and
the Missouri River from the north pushed into the area. Dakota
was part of the lands drained by the Mississippi River that had

This lead plate was buried by the La Vérendrye brothers near present-day Pierre in 1743.

been claimed for France in 1682 by René-Robert Cavelier, Sieur de La Salle. This territory was called Louisiana. Between 1683 and 1700, French fur traders from the Minnesota area carried on limited trade with Indians in present-day South Dakota.

The first known exploration of the region did not take place, however, until 1742. That year, Louis Joseph and François La Vérendrye, looking for a water route to the Pacific, left Canada and followed the Missouri River south to the site of present-day Fort Pierre. In 1913, a lead plate that they had buried there in 1743 was discovered by three children while playing. The La Vérendrye expedition opened the Upper Missouri Valley to the French fur trade. Indians exchanged fur pelts for metal pots, pans, and tools.

In 1762, during the French and Indian War, France turned over the Louisiana lands to Spain. With France's defeat in 1763, Britain gained control of French lands in Canada and east of the Mississippi. British fur traders began trading in the Dakota region illegally. To protect their interests in the area, Spanish officials in St. Louis sent fur traders, most of them French, into Dakota. From 1794 to 1796, Jean Baptiste Trudeau tried to establish trade with the Arikara, Mandan, and Sioux. Because these Indian tribes were waging warfare against one another, Trudeau returned to St. Louis with fewer furs than expected.

In 1800, French Emperor Napoleon Bonaparte forced Spain to sign a secret treaty returning the Louisiana region to France. In 1803, needing money to finance his European wars, Napoleon sold the territory to the United States for $15 million. The Louisiana Purchase doubled the size of the young nation, which had won its independence from Britain in 1783. The United States now owned the land of the Sioux and Arikara. However, the fact that white men had been exchanging control of the land meant little to the Indians, who believed land could not be owned.

AMERICAN EXPLORERS, TRADERS, AND TRAVELERS

Within a year of acquiring the Louisiana Purchase, President Jefferson sent an expedition, headed by Captain Meriwether Lewis and Lieutenant William Clark, to explore the new territory. Leaving St. Louis in May 1804, they followed the Missouri River north. On August 22, they made camp near present-day Elk Point in South Dakota's southeastern corner.

Altogether, the expedition spent sixty-nine days in what is now South Dakota. Lewis and Clark established friendly terms with the Arikara and Yankton Sioux, but had to deal firmly with the more hostile Teton Sioux. Their journals provide detailed information about the Indian tribes, soil, climate, plants, animals, and minerals of the region.

In the years following the expedition, more fur traders, trappers, and hunters entered the region and established trading posts on the Missouri, James, Vermillion, and Big Sioux rivers. Large trading companies, such as the American Fur Company and the Columbia Fur Company, controlled most of this trade. Through a law that had been passed in 1802, Congress regulated trade with the Indians in Dakota.

During the War of 1812, the United States used fur trader Manuel Lisa to win the Sioux's friendship and to wrest the fur trade from the British, who were still operating illegally in the area. Lisa built two forts, one on the present North Dakota-South Dakota border, and another near the Big Bend of the Missouri, between present-day Pierre and Chamberlain. With Britain's defeat in 1814, control of Dakota and the fur trade was firmly in American hands.

In 1817, French trader Joseph La Framboise established a trading post that became the region's first permanent white settlement. Located at the mouth of the Bad River, the trading post was rebuilt as Fort Tecumseh in 1822. In 1832, it was renamed Fort Pierre after Pierre Chouteau, Jr., the western agent for the American Fur Company. The fort served as headquarters for the region's fur trade and for travelers on the Missouri.

Travel for traders, trappers, and soldiers became easier, faster, and safer when steamboats replaced keelboats for the voyage upriver. In 1831, the *Yellowstone*, owned by Chouteau, made its first trip to Fort Tecumseh, carrying goods to be traded for furs and buffalo hides. The following year, the *Yellowstone* carried artist George Catlin to Fort Pierre, where he painted a Teton Sioux encampment. Other steamboat travelers included German Prince Maximilian and Karl Bodmer, a Swiss artist who illustrated *Maximilian's Travels in the Interior of North America*. In 1843, John James Audubon painted birds and other animals that he observed along the way.

Priests and ministers also entered Dakota. In 1839, Father Pierre Jean De Smet arrived by steamboat at the mouth of the Vermillion

Fort Pierre as it appeared in the 1800s

River. From 1849 to 1873, he ministered to the Teton Sioux in the Black Hills. When they showed him gold pieces found in the hills, he wisely advised them not to let white men know about their find. In 1840, Stephen Return Riggs, a Protestant missionary from the Minnesota region, did work among the Indians around Fort Pierre.

During the 1850s, the fur trade began to decline. The number of pelts decreased and beaver hats, once the height of fashion for men in the East, were replaced by silk top hats. With the passing of the fur trade, Chouteau sold Fort Pierre to the United States Army in 1855. Soldiers were stationed there to keep peace between the Sioux and the white settlers and traders. In 1856, General William S. Harney began supervising the construction of Fort Randall. Located on the west bank of the Missouri just north of the present border with Nebraska, this fort symbolized the army's control over the northern Great Plains.

Chapter 5
PIONEER DAYS

PIONEER DAYS

INDIAN LANDS AND NEW SETTLEMENTS

In 1851, under pressure from the United States government, the Santee Sioux gave up all land east of the Big Sioux River. Then, in 1858, Captain John B. S. Todd, a Yankton trading-post operator and cousin of Mary Todd Lincoln, negotiated a treaty with the Yankton Sioux. They yielded land between the Big Sioux and the Missouri south of a line from Fort Pierre to present-day Watertown. Both tribes moved to reservations—the Santee to one on the Minnesota River near Big Stone Lake; the Yankton to one on the Missouri River south of Fort Randall. In exchange, the government promised the Indians protection, food, education, and health care.

Early visitors to Dakota called the region the "Great American Desert," believing that the land was unfit for farming or settlement. Land companies, however, quickly began buying parcels of the newly ceded land. In 1857, Minnesota and Iowa companies chose rival townsites at Sioux Falls because the area had building stone, plenty of timber, and fertile land for farming. In addition, the falls of the Big Sioux River could provide power for mills. Sioux Falls developers immediately began to push for territorial status for the Dakota region. When the land ceded by the Yankton Sioux officially came under government control in 1859, a thousand settlers rushed across the Iowa and present-day

Chief Red Cloud (right), shown here with another Sioux leader, American Horse, fought to stop the building of a federal road through Indian hunting grounds in Dakota Territory.

Nebraska borders. The new settlers established the towns of Bon Homme, Vermillion, and Yankton. People in Yankton also wanted territorial status for Dakota, with Yankton as the capital.

On March 2, 1861, President James Buchanan signed the bill that set up Dakota Territory. With Yankton as its capital, the new territory included the present states of North Dakota and South Dakota, as well as most of Montana and Wyoming. John B. S. Todd became the territory's first delegate to Congress.

An 1862 Santee Sioux uprising in Minnesota spread into the Dakota Territory and lasted until 1866. This, combined with droughts in 1864 and 1865, caused half of the settlers to leave the territory. Sioux Falls stood abandoned for two years, and Yankton was the only settlement left in the east. Within a few years, however, many of the settlers had returned.

The discovery of gold in Montana in the early 1860s brought thousands of miners from the East through Dakota. Some Dakotans worked quickly to get federal money for building roads to the goldfields. In 1866, the army started to make a survey for a road through Indian hunting grounds in the Powder River area in Wyoming. Oglala Sioux Chief Red Cloud objected and had his warriors attack the troops. The Indian raids that collectively became known as Chief Red Cloud's War continued for several years. In 1868, to end the raids, the government signed the Laramie Treaty, which met the Indians' demands. Through this treaty, the government abandoned its posts in the area, halted its plans for roads, and guaranteed to the Teton Sioux all land west of the Missouri River in present-day South Dakota—creating the Great Sioux Reservation.

With the decline of the fur trade and with most of the buffalo herds destroyed by over-hunting, the Indians could no longer support themselves. By 1868, most of the Sioux who had lived east of the Missouri had moved onto reservations. They now depended on the United States government for food and supplies.

GROWTH IN THE TERRITORY

With most of the Indians on reservations, the southeastern part of Dakota Territory once again looked attractive to farmers and entrepreneurs. Settlements sprouted up farther north on the Big Sioux River and north of Vermillion and Yankton on the Vermillion and James rivers. The completion of the Sioux City and Pacific Railroad to Sioux City, Iowa, in 1868, provided the area's farmers with a way to transport their wheat to eastern markets. By 1869, bridges had been constructed across the Vermillion and James rivers as part of a road from Sioux City to Fort Randall, making it easier to reach the railroad at Sioux City. When the Dakota Southern Railroad, between Sioux City and Yankton, opened in 1873, the area attracted more settlers, and Yankton became an important river port.

Between 1868 and 1873, Swedish, Danish, and Czech immigrants arrived in the territory, most of them through Sioux

The Dakota Southern Railroad's *Black Hills No. 1*, the first locomotive to reach Yankton, arrived in late 1872.

City, Iowa. In 1871, the territorial legislature set up an immigration bureau to encourage immigrants to settle in the territory. From 1873 to 1877, German Mennonites (a Protestant sect that stresses pacifism and simple living) and Hutterites (a related sect that practices communal living) emigrated from Russia. These immigrant farmers adapted their techniques to the Dakota prairies and built farms on land previously thought unsuitable for agriculture.

LIFE ON THE PRAIRIE

In the 1850s and 1860s, pioneers entered Dakota in covered wagons or on steamboats. By the 1870s, many were arriving on the newly constructed railroad. No matter how they traveled, they brought few possessions with them. Clothing, bedding, kitchen utensils, a few pieces of furniture, tools, lumber, and farm equipment made up their baggage. Before 1862, these pioneers acquired public land under the pre-emption law, which allowed them to purchase 160 acres (65 hectares) for $1.25 per acre. After Congress passed the Homestead Act in 1862, pioneers could claim

The "soddy," the most common type of dwelling for early South Dakota settlers, was made of thick strips of sod piled like bricks.

the same amount of land for free if they lived on and improved the land for five years.

The first order of business for these pioneers was building a home. Because trees were scarce on the prairie, most settlers constructed pine-board-and-tar-paper shanties or sod houses. The walls of a "soddy" were made of thick strips of sod that were piled like bricks. Openings were left for a door and windows. A few sod houses had wooden roofs, but most had sod roofs. The sod provided insulation against heat and cold, but was damp during rainy weather and could collapse in heavy rain. After several good years of farming, a family might be able to build a frame house.

To farm the land, settlers used a special plow to break through the thick prairie sod. During the first summer, a farmer might raise sod corn (for cattle feed), potatoes, onions, beets, beans, and other vegetables. In following years, after the soil had been reworked, he could plant wheat and other grain crops.

The interior of a typical South Dakota pioneer soddy of the late 1880s

Each season held its own threat of disaster on the prairie. Winter blizzards, such as the one during the "long winter" of 1880-81, isolated farm families and small towns from sources of food and fuel. In the spring and fall, prairie fires swept across the dry grasses, destroying fields of crops, animals, homes, and whole towns in their paths. Summer often brought drought and plagues of grasshoppers. If lack of rain did not kill the crops in the fields, hordes of grasshoppers might swarm over entire farms and devour the crops. Only the hardiest people stayed in the Dakota Territory.

BLACK HILLS GOLD

While settlers in East River Country were establishing farming communities, miners and prospectors made plans to enter the sacred Sioux ground, the Black Hills, in search of gold. Most of the Teton Sioux in the area had not settled down to an agricultural life on the Great Sioux Reservation but continued to rove through the countryside in bands. To keep white settlers out of the area as spelled out in the treaty and to contain the Sioux, the government decided to build a fort in the Black Hills. In 1874, Lieutenant Colonel George A. Custer led an expedition of more than a thousand men into the Black Hills. This force was to locate a site for a fort and to gather information about the region's soil, minerals, and plant and animal life.

Miners with the expedition found gold near the present town of Custer in July 1874. Instantly, newspaper headlines in St. Paul and Chicago shouted the news of the Black Hills gold find. Within a year, more than eight hundred miners had entered the region illegally. Realizing that it was now impossible to keep miners out of the Hills, the government tried to negotiate with the Sioux, offering them $6 million for the Black Hills. Even though there were few buffalo left in the Hills and the land could not be farmed, the Sioux refused all offers because the Black Hills were sacred to them. At that point, the army withdrew from the region, leaving the miners on their own.

In the spring of 1876, Oglala Chief Crazy Horse, Hunkpapa medicine man Sitting Bull, and Brûlé Chief Spotted Tail gathered west of the Black Hills and prepared for what became known as the Sioux War of 1876. Attacks on mining camps occurred sporadically throughout the year. Most of the fighting, however, took place between the army and the Sioux in the Montana and Wyoming regions, including the famous Battle of the Little Big Horn in Montana, also known as Custer's Last Stand.

The only battle in Dakota Territory occurred in September at Slim Buttes. There, the United States army destroyed the camp of Sioux leader American Horse and his men, then held off a counterattack by Crazy Horse's forces. In October, the Sioux

Deadwood in 1876

agreed to give up the Black Hills, as well as a 50-mile (80-kilometer) strip of land to the east. Sitting Bull fled to Canada, while most of the Brûlé Sioux moved to reservation land near Rosebud Creek. The Oglala Sioux settled on reservation land at Pine Ridge near the Nebraska border. Crazy Horse was killed in Nebraska while being arrested.

Before the Sioux War started, the towns of Custer, Hill City, Rapid City, Deadwood, Lead (pronounced "leed"), Rockerville, and Spearfish had already been founded. With the Black Hills now safe after Indian withdrawal, more miners rushed into the area. At the height of the gold rush, in 1877, more than twenty-five thousand people populated the Hills. Many of them were miners who had been in on the California, Montana, and Colorado gold rushes. More than a hundred Chinese from California settled in Deadwood, panning for gold or operating laundries, restaurants, and grocery stores. With its one main street lined tightly with saloons and gambling houses, Deadwood gained the reputation as

Workers at the famous Homestake Mine in Lead

the wildest, most lawless town in the West. "Wild Bill" Hickok met his end there when, while playing poker, he was shot in the back of the head by Jack McCall. The hand that he dropped—two black aces, two black eights, and the nine of diamonds—is now known as the "dead man's hand."

In the streams around Custer and Deadwood, prospectors panned for loose flakes, grains, and nuggets of gold. Where water was scarce, such as at Rockerville, miners used wooden boxes on rockers to sift out the gold. At "leads"—outcroppings of rock containing gold—shafts were quickly sunk for following the veins underground. A lead found by Moses and Fred Manual and Henry Harney in 1876 led to the founding of the Homestake Mining Company, now the largest gold mine in the Western Hemisphere, and still very much in operation in Lead.

THE GREAT DAKOTA BOOM

With the opening of the Black Hills, cattle ranchers as well as miners moved into the area. Young Texas longhorn steers were

Ranching began to take hold in western South Dakota in the late 1870s.

driven "on hoof" from Texas to graze on the buffalo grass of the
open range around the Black Hills. During this same time, sheep
ranching began to take hold in the western part of Dakota
Territory as well. Because cattle ranchers believed that the sheep
ate the grass down to the ground, leaving nothing for the cattle, a
range war developed between sheep and cattle ranchers.

By 1884, about eight hundred thousand head of cattle and
eighty-five thousand sheep were grazing on the open range. In the
early years, range animals were butchered in South Dakota; the
meat was then sold to miners in the Black Hills, homesteaders,
and townspeople. When railroads reached Rapid City from
Nebraska in the 1880s, cattle and sheep began being shipped to
slaughterhouses in Omaha, Chicago, and other eastern cities. The
railroads brought into the region homesteaders who planned to

This 1890s advertisement for the Chicago & North Western Railroad prodded people to take advantage of such newly accessible parts of the Midwest as South Dakota.

farm. Dividing up the grazing land into smaller fenced farms brought an end to the open-range system.

Railroad building also benefited the East River region. The Chicago & North Western and the Chicago, Milwaukee, & St. Paul railroads extended their lines from Minnesota to the Missouri River and brought a new wave of settlers to Dakota. Watertown, Aberdeen, Brookings, De Smet, Huron, Pierre, Mitchell, and Chamberlain were all founded as railroad towns between 1879 and 1881.

Although many industries were established during the 1880s and 1890s, only 1 percent of the population were industrial workers in 1899. Flour milling, the territory's major industry, flourished along the Big Sioux, Vermillion, and James rivers. Brick making was done in Rapid City and Yankton. Yankton also had a cement plant. The gypsum plant in Hot Springs provided material for stucco and wall plaster. Quarrying of red quartzite near Sioux Falls and Dell Rapids led to the opening of a stone-polishing works.

THE MOVE FOR STATEHOOD

With the great population increase of the 1870s and 1880s, territorial officials began to petition Congress for statehood. One group wanted one state created from the Dakota Territory; another group pushed for separate statehood for North Dakota and South Dakota. In 1883, a constitution for South Dakota was drawn up, and a delegation went to Washington, D.C. Because both regions of the Dakota Territory were heavily Republican, the Democrat-controlled House of Representatives ignored the petition for statehood. Another constitution was written and approved in 1885, but statehood was again denied.

When the Republican party made the admission of two states an issue in the 1888 presidential campaign, and then won a healthy number of seats in Congress, South Dakota's statehood was assured. The Democrats in Congress shifted their position, and in February 1889, Congress set the current boundary between North Dakota and South Dakota. On October 1, the people of South Dakota reapproved the 1885 constitution, elected Arthur Mellette as governor, and chose Pierre as the state's capital. When President Benjamin Harrison signed a proclamation on November 2 admitting both North Dakota and South Dakota to the Union, the documents were shuffled so that no one could tell which state had been admitted first. By alphabetical order, North Dakota became the thirty-ninth state; South Dakota became the fortieth.

Chapter 6
THE
CENTENNIAL
YEARS

THE CENTENNIAL YEARS

*My father no longer wrestles a team of horses and a clumsy
wagon to haul dirt. He directs a crew . . . outfitted with
trucks and tractors . . . and powerful cranes in the
maintenance of parks and grounds around Gavins Point Dam.
Still, he works hard. . . . Hard work is a legacy of the
generations who settled the prairie, broke the soil, built
the sod houses, fought the droughts and grasshoppers and
penny-a-pound prices for their products.*
—news anchor Tom Brokaw

THE SIOUX'S LAST STAND

During the first years of South Dakota's statehood, the West
River Country experienced many changes. After 1876, when the
Sioux surrendered the Black Hills, ranchers and farmers began
settling on the 50-mile (80-kilometer) strip of land east of the
Black Hills. However, because the land between the Missouri
River and this western white settlement was still Indian territory,
no roads or railroads could be built to link the East River Country
with the West River Country. In 1889, to avoid further fighting,
some Sioux chiefs grudgingly ceded the land west of the Missouri
to the federal government and moved to the Standing Rock,
Cheyenne River, Pine Ridge, and Rosebud reservations. When the
government failed to live up to its promises by cutting the
Indians' beef rations and not increasing educational programs, the
Sioux felt they had once again been tricked by the white
government.

By 1890, the Teton Sioux had become part of a religious

Casualties of
the 1890 massacre
at Wounded Knee

movement, called the Ghost Dance, that was started in present-day Nevada by a Paiute Indian named Wovoka. Followers of the Ghost Dance movement believed that performing this dance would cause the whites to vanish, the Indians to regain the land, and the buffalo herds to return. While performing the frenzied Ghost Dance, which was forbidden by the government, the Sioux wore white shirts that they believed would protect them from soldiers' bullets.

The Ghost Dance movement made non-Indians uneasy, and the federal government, fearing another Sioux uprising, attempted to stop it. In December 1890, Sitting Bull (who had returned to South Dakota and settled on the Standing Rock Reservation in 1883) was killed while being arrested by reservation police. About a hundred of Sitting Bull's followers fled from the Standing Rock Reservation. Intending to hide in the Badlands, they joined a body of ghost dancers led by ailing Chief Big Foot. The entire group surrendered, however, when stopped by troops of the 7th Cavalry, who then marched them to Wounded Knee Creek. While the soldiers were disarming the Sioux (who actually were carrying only a few outdated rifles), a shot rang out. In response, the soldiers opened fire, indiscriminately killing more than two hundred Indian men, women, and children. Those Indians who tried to escape into a nearby ravine were hunted and gunned down.

The Wounded Knee Massacre was the last major armed conflict between Indians and the United States Army. Buried at Wounded Knee were not only the bodies of the Sioux, but also the last hope of the American Indians to regain their old way of life.

A SLOW START FOR THE NEW STATE

Between 1889 and 1897, severe drought discouraged settlement in newly opened Indian lands west of the Missouri. By 1900, however, better weather conditions and good prices for crops brought thousands of new settlers into the state. The federal government opened more new Indian lands in the west, and people could win parcels of this land through a lottery. Between 1900 and 1910, nearly ninety-four thousand people homesteaded in the West River Country.

No longer hindered by Indian territory, the North Western and the Milwaukee railroads bridged the Missouri River at Pierre and Chamberlain, respectively. By 1910, their lines extended to Rapid City. At the same time, the Milwaukee continued its line from Aberdeen to Lemmon by building a bridge across the Missouri at Mobridge.

South Dakota's twentieth-century West River pioneers were less prepared to deal with the harsh climate and land than East River pioneers of the 1800s had been. When drought hit again in 1910 and 1911, many homesteaders left the state. Those who stayed adapted their farming techniques to the land by rotating crops, raising cattle and sheep, and growing grain crops for feeding cattle.

EARLY STATE POLITICS

During these early years of statehood, South Dakotans elected
reformers from the Populist and Progressive Republican parties to
state offices. Their programs were aimed at protecting the rights
and improving the lives of South Dakotans. In 1898, the state
legislature passed the first initiative and referendum law in the
nation. Initiative allows voters to pass laws directly if they obtain
enough petition signatures to get a suggested law on the ballot.
Through referendum, 5 percent of the voters can request a vote by
the people to reject laws passed by the legislature.

Progressive legislation enacted between 1907 and 1918 included
laws establishing direct primary elections, a maximum passenger
rate on the railroads, and free textbooks in public schools. The
Progressives also set up state hail insurance for farmers, a way for
farmers to obtain loans from the state, and a law guaranteeing the
safety of bank deposits.

WORLD WARS AND THE DEPRESSION

The United States' entry into World War I in 1917 brought
prosperity to South Dakota. Prices for crops and livestock rose, the
amount of farm products increased, and the value of farmland
doubled because of wartime demands. South Dakotans also served
the war effort in other ways. More than 32,000 served in the army,
and 310 died in battle or later from wounds.

South Dakota's commendable war record was marred, however,
by its treatment of citizens with German backgrounds. Wartime
hysteria caused some South Dakotans—as it did many
Americans—to question these people's loyalty to the United
States. The pacifist Hutterites, who did not believe in war, refused

South Dakotans
signing up for Works
Progress Administration
(WPA) jobs during
the Great Depression
of the 1930s

to support the war effort. When some Hutterite property was
seized by local defense councils and sold for contributions to the
war, many of the Hutterites moved to Canada.

After the war ended, prices for farm products fell and the value
of land declined. Many farmers, having less farm income, lost
their farms because they were unable to pay their debts. Many
South Dakotans left the state to find work elsewhere. When the
New York Stock Market crashed in 1929, plunging the entire
nation into the greatest depression in its history, South Dakotans
were already suffering. During the 1930s, nearly ten years of
drought, grasshopper plagues, dust storms, and crop failures
added to their misery.

The New Deal programs of President Franklin D. Roosevelt,
who took office in 1933, brought some relief to South Dakotans.
When the government increased the price of gold, mining revived
in the Black Hills. The government also bought cattle and sheep,
which were processed at South Dakota's meat-packing plants.
Some farmers were relocated to more productive land and taught
how to conserve the soil by planting drought-resistant
shortgrasses. More than twenty-five thousand young men

received jobs with the Civilian Conservation Corps (CCC). Most worked in the Black Hills, planting trees and building recreational facilities. The Works Progress Administration (WPA) spent over $35 million helping South Dakotans build schools and other public buildings, bridges, and roads.

America's entry into World War II, which occurred after Japan bombed Pearl Harbor on December 7, 1941, brought South Dakota and the rest of the nation out of the depression. War once again brought prosperity, since meat, poultry, milk, and grain products were much needed for the war effort. More than 64,000 South Dakotans served in the armed forces in the Pacific, North Africa, and Italy.

The wartime building of the Sioux Falls Air Force Training Base, Ellsworth Air Base outside Rapid City, and an ordnance depot at Provo boosted the state's economy. Machine shops and foundries popped up all over the state. When the government ordered gold mining to cease, the mining companies mined materials such as coal, tungsten, bentonite, feldspar, and mica for the war effort.

POSTWAR PROSPERITY

Prosperity continued for South Dakotans after World War II. Farm income rose, many farmers were able to buy back farms they had lost in the depression, and better roads made it easier for farmers to market their produce. Farm-related manufacturing boomed, and the state-owned cement plant at Rapid City, founded in 1924, enjoyed its greatest period of prosperity. In spite of this progress, many young people continued to leave the state when they could not find work in the towns.

To improve the state's economy and make it less dependent on farming, the state and federal governments devised a plan to develop the Missouri River and its tributaries. Dams were built on the Cheyenne, Grand, and Moreau rivers and on Rapid Creek for flood control and irrigation. Recreational facilities for swimming and boating were later built at the reservoirs.

Between 1946 and 1966, the Missouri River was dammed at four places to provide electric power, flood control, irrigation, recreational facilities, and habitats for fish and wildlife. The dams' power plants supply electricity, while the reservoirs furnish water for irrigating farmland, mainly in central South Dakota. Created by damming the Missouri, the "Great Lakes of South Dakota"—Oahe, Francis Case, Sharpe, and Lewis and Clark — attract tourists to the state and in general have improved the state's economy. However, the lakes permanently flooded some of the best farmland, including some on Indian reservations, causing new reasons for bitterness.

RECENT DEVELOPMENTS

South Dakota's severe weather has continued to deal harsh blows to the state. Blizzards in 1966 and 1975 claimed several human lives and thousands of cattle. When heavy rains caused the Canyon Lake Dam to burst in 1972, floodwaters swept through Rapid City, killing 238 people and causing $100 million in property damage.

In 1988, a drought severely damaged South Dakota's wheat, rye, and corn crops. The heat and strong winds also produced dust storms. These extremely dry conditions led to disaster in the Black Hills National Forest. Lightning struck on July 5, causing a wildfire that destroyed 16,788 acres (6,794 hectares) of timber, valued at $4.4 million. Fighting the fire cost about $2 million, but millions more were lost in tourist dollars as roads into the Black Hills had to be closed. Problems with relations between the Sioux

During the drought that hit much of the nation in 1988, dangerously dry conditions resulted in a terrible fire in the Black Hills National Forest.

and the federal government resurfaced in the 1970s. In 1973, members of the American Indian Movement (AIM), a militant civil rights group, seized the village of Wounded Knee to protest the leadership on the Pine Ridge Reservation and to demand an investigation of the Bureau of Indian Affairs' policies toward all tribes. The occupation ended seventy-one days later, after two deaths and 300 arrests. Members of the Sioux then began working with the government to improve Indian education and expand tribal industries. In 1979, the U.S. Supreme Court ordered the government to pay the Sioux $122.5 million for land in the Black Hills that had been seized in 1876. The dispute continues, however, as the Sioux have refused the money, seeking no less than full return of the land.

During the 1980s, nationwide cuts in federal spending for housing, job training, loans to small businesses, and education hit South Dakota especially hard. Unemployment on the reservations reached 80%. Farm incomes fell because of low prices for farm products and high interest rates for mortgages. A few farmers sold their farms, while many others lost their land through foreclosure.

In 1987, the state government started a program to encourage the growth of business and industry. One of the goals was to create jobs for both Indian and non-Indian residents. In addition, a $40 million fund was established to grant low-interest loans to new and expanding businesses.

State officials and the Bureau of Indian Affairs are now trying to develop job opportunities on the reservations. For example, the mining of a mineral called zeolite, and the milling of zeolite for fertilizer, have provided jobs on the Pine Ridge Reservation.

In 1989, South Dakota held a year-long celebration of its first 100 years of statehood. Many activities highlighted the state and its history. On August 29, two wagon trains — one setting out from Elk Point in the East River Country and the other from Philip in the West River region — met at the Centennial State Fair in Huron.

As South Dakotans honored the 19th-century pioneers, they also looked forward to a second century that would bring harmony and prosperity for all of the state's people. Governor George Mickelson declared 1990 a "year of reconciliation," and called for Indians and non-Indians all over South Dakota to learn about each other's culture, and to live together in peace and cooperation. One result of their effort is that while most of the United States celebrates Columbus Day each October, the people of South Dakota have renamed that holiday Native American Day.

In 1991, Governor Mickelson expanded the original idea, calling for a "century of reconciliation." Now Indians and non-Indians from all areas of society in South Dakota — schools, businesses, big cities, small towns, and reservations — meet each other to help foster better communication, friendship, understanding, and good will.

Chapter 7

GOVERNMENT AND THE ECONOMY

SOVTH DAKOTA

GOVERNMENT AND THE ECONOMY

GOVERNMENT

South Dakota's government is based on its original constitution, which was adopted October 1, 1889. Since then, South Dakotans have amended the constitution more than eighty times. Like the United States Constitution, South Dakota's constitution divides the state's government into three branches: executive, legislative, and judicial.

The governor, who heads the executive branch, is elected to a four-year term, and may serve no more than two consecutive terms. The same is true of the lieutenant governor. Other elected officials in the executive branch are the attorney general, secretary of state, auditor, treasurer, and commissioner of school and public lands. They serve four-year terms as well, but may be reelected any number of times. The governor appoints the superintendent of schools, as well as many other officials, and can call special sessions of the legislature.

South Dakota's legislative branch consists of a thirty-five-member senate and a seventy-member house of representatives. Members of both houses of the legislature are elected to two-year terms. The legislature passes bills, then sends them to the governor. When the governor signs a bill, it becomes law. If the governor vetoes a bill, it is returned to the legislature. With enough votes, the legislature can then pass the bill into law over the governor's veto.

The judicial branch consists of the state's court system. The state supreme court is the highest court in South Dakota. Its five justices are elected to eight-year terms. The justices elect their own chief justice. Below the supreme court is the circuit court, with thirty-six judges spread over eight judicial districts. Nineteen county court districts and municipal courts in Sioux Falls, Rapid City, and Aberdeen are also part of the judicial system. The judges in all of these courts are elected.

South Dakota's local government is administered through its 66 counties, 310 incorporated towns and cities, and 1,050 organized townships. Maintaining schools, roads, and law-enforcement agencies and providing for soil conservation and drainage are a few of the services provided by local governments.

Governmental services are paid for through a sales tax; a general property tax; automobile and truck license fees; additional taxes on motor fuels, tobacco, and alcoholic beverages; and federal grants. South Dakota does not tax personal property or income. Banks and other financial institutions, however, pay a corporate tax. All these taxes and fees help South Dakota operate on a balanced budget. Because the state constitution prohibits deficit spending, the state cannot spend more money than it takes in.

EDUCATION

Since the early days of settlement, South Dakotans have given education top priority. Today, South Dakota has one of the highest literacy rates in the nation. According to state law, children between the ages of seven and sixteen must attend school.

Today's schools have come a long way from the log-and-sod buildings of the 1800s. Most of South Dakota's 102,000 elementary

The University of South Dakota in Vermillion is the state's oldest public university.

and 36,000 secondary students now attend the state's 915 large, well-equipped schools. However, 83 schools with just one teacher and 48 schools with only two teachers continue to operate in the state. Most of those schools are in isolated parts of western South Dakota. In addition to the regular public schools, the state also maintains a school for the visually impaired, in Aberdeen; schools for the deaf, in Sioux Falls; and schools for the developmentally disabled, in Redfield and Custer.

Religious groups operate two Indian schools in the state. The Jesuits educate Oglala Sioux children at the Red Cloud Indian School near Pine Ridge. Chamberlain's St. Joseph's Indian School keeps the Sioux heritage alive while providing a well-rounded education to first graders through eighth graders. The school also helps Indian businesses and craftspeople market their traditionally designed products.

The Bureau of Indian Affairs (BIA), a federal agency that is part

A cattle drive in the Black Hills

of the Department of the Interior, runs twenty-one schools, including some boarding schools, for Indian students in South Dakota. All are located on or very near reservations.

South Dakota is proud of its fourteen degree-granting colleges and universities and its four vocational-technical institutes. In 1882, the college that was to become the University of South Dakota was founded in Vermillion. South Dakota State University, founded a year later in Brookings as an agricultural college, has a graduate school and schools of education, engineering, nursing, and pharmacy. Other state-run schools include South Dakota School of Mines and Technology in Rapid City, Black Hills State University in Spearfish, Northern State University in Aberdeen, and Dakota State University in Madison. Oglala Lakota College in Kyle and Sinte Gleska College in Rosebud are tribally run, federally funded community colleges that provide higher education for the Sioux.

Private colleges in South Dakota include Mount Marty College, in Yankton; Augustana College and Sioux Falls College, in Sioux Falls; Dakota Wesleyan University, in Mitchell; Huron College, in Huron, and Presentation College, in Aberdeen.

AGRICULTURE

South Dakota's economy is based mainly on producing, processing, and transporting agricultural products. Livestock products and crops provide 11 percent of South Dakota's gross state product (GSP), the total value of goods and services produced annually. In no other state does agriculture account for such a high percentage of the state's economic output.

Beef and dairy cattle, hogs, lambs, sheep, chickens, turkeys, and geese—along with their by-products of meat, hides, wool, milk, and eggs—yield 68 percent of farm and ranch income. Ranches in the west produce most of the state's beef cattle and sheep. Eastern farms raise most of the state's dairy cattle and poultry. South Dakota ranks first in the nation in the production of geese, fourth in lambs, fifth in sheep and beef cattle, and seventh in calves. Belle Fourche, on the northern edge of the Black Hills, is the nation's number-one wool market and a leading cattle market. The Sioux Falls Stockyards hold daily auctions for cattle, pigs, sheep, and lambs.

The other 32 percent of South Dakota's farm income comes from crops. Corn and wheat are the state's largest crops. Most of the corn is grown in the southeast. Spring wheat is produced mainly in the north, and winter wheat thrives in the southwest. South Dakota, however, ranks first in the nation in the production of rye, second in flaxseed and sunflowers, third in oats, fourth in honey, sixth in winter wheat and spring wheat, seventh in

Wheat (left) and sorghum (right) are two of South Dakota's leading agricultural products.

sorghum, and ninth in corn. Much of the corn provides feed for hogs and cattle. In many years, the state produces half of the country's supply of bluegrass seed. The land also yields large amounts of soybeans.

MANUFACTURING

South Dakota's 750 manufacturing and processing plants provide 9 percent of the gross state product and employ about 10 percent of the state's workers. Food processing and the manufacture of lumber, wood products, and industrial machinery are the state's most important manufacturing activities.

The food-processing industry, based on the state's agricultural production, is the leading manufacturing activity. Meat processing and packing plants in Sioux Falls, Huron, and Rapid City produce fresh meat, canned and whole hams, sausages, and hot dogs. Milk and milk products flow from creameries and dairy-processing

Most of the lumber produced in South Dakota comes from the forests of the Black Hills.

plants in Aberdeen, Mitchell, Rapid City, and Sioux Falls. Watertown has a poultry-processing plant, and Rapid City has a flour mill.

South Dakota's second-leading manufacturing activity is the production of nonelectrical machinery. Rapid City and Sioux Falls are centers for manufacturing farm and construction machinery. Aircraft parts, boats, bus bodies, and truck trailers are also made in the state. Skilled workers make surgical instruments in factories in Aberdeen and Brookings. Some of South Dakota's other manufactured products include hot-air balloons, electronic components, textiles, clothing, leather goods, and Sioux pottery. Artistic jewelers craft Black Hills gold into delicate grapevine-design jewelry.

In the Black Hills, lumbering is an important industry. Ponderosa pine is used for pulpwood and for construction posts and poles. Other woods are used for cabinet and furniture making. The lumber companies replace the trees that they cut down by planting seedlings.

Black Hills gold, shown here in bar form (left) and being crafted into fine jewelry (right), is South Dakota's most important mineral.

MINING

Black Hills gold, the state's most important mineral, accounts for over half of South Dakota's mining income. The Homestake Mine in Lead, the largest gold-producing mine in the Western Hemisphere, yields more than 300,000 troy ounces of gold a year. Altogether, Homestake and South Dakota's other mines produce about 360,000 troy ounces a year. About $500,000 worth of silver is mined each year in South Dakota, most of it from the Homestake Mine.

Petroleum, the state's second-most important mineral, is mined in north-central and western South Dakota. Mineral products quarried in the state include granite, crushed stone, sand, and gravel. Six granite quarries in northeastern South Dakota near Milbank provide 30 percent of the deep red granite used for

The Homestake Mine in Lead is the largest gold-producing mine in the Western Hemisphere.

monuments in the United States. Most of the state's limestone, crushed stone, sand, and gravel comes from the eastern part of the state and from the Black Hills. These products are important for cement production in Rapid City and for road-building and other construction projects throughout the state.

Other minerals found in South Dakota include zeolite, mica, feldspar, gypsum, natural gas, uranium, and bentonite. Bentonite, mined near Belle Fourche, is called the clay of a thousand uses. Clay bricks, dynamite, crayons, face cream, and paper are just a few of the many items in which bentonite is used.

SERVICE INDUSTRIES

Nearly three-fourths of South Dakota's GSP is generated by service industries. Thirty-two percent of the state's approximately two hundred thousand service industry workers are employed in the fields of wholesale and retail trades, banking, insurance, or real estate.

Community, social, personal, and government services employ about 30 percent of those involved in service industries. South Dakota's public schools and hospitals, military bases, Indian reservations, national parks and forests, and state parks and recreation areas are a few of the places that utilize government workers.

Ellsworth Air Force Base, outside Rapid City; and the Air Force's Strategic Training Radar Complex, west of Belle Fourche, are part of the nation's defense system. About 350 scientists and technically trained employees work at the United States Department of the Interior's Earth Resources Observation Systems (EROS) Data Center northeast of Sioux Falls. At EROS, photographs of the earth, taken from airplanes and satellites and used for studying the earth and its resources, are processed.

Tourism uses the skills of workers from many of the state's service industries. Tourists spend more than $500 million a year in South Dakota on food, lodging, transportation, and entertainment.

TRANSPORTATION AND COMMUNICATION

South Dakota has more than 73,000 miles (117,479 kilometers) of roads, 80 percent of which are paved. Interstates 29 and 90 link South Dakota to the rest of the nation. Interstate 29 provides a north-south route near the state's eastern border. Interstate 90 runs east and west across the southern third of the state.

About 3,000 miles (4,828 kilometers) of railroad track serve the six railroads that provide freight service in South Dakota.

Tourism is an important aspect of South Dakota's economy.

Passenger railroads no longer service the state. Commercial airlines operate from the state's nine major airports, the largest of which are in Sioux Falls and Rapid City. There are also seventy public and eighty private airfields around the state.

Throughout the state, thirteen daily and about ninety weekly newspapers are published. Sioux Falls' *Argus Leader* and the *Rapid City Journal* have the largest daily circulations. Established as the *Weekly Dakotian* in 1861, the daily *Yankton Press and Dakotan* is the state's longest-running newspaper.

South Dakota has about sixty-five radio stations and nineteen television stations, including eight public broadcasting channels. In 1922, the state's first radio station, WCAT, broadcast from Rapid City under the direction of the South Dakota School of Mines and Technology. KELO, the state's first television station, went on the air in Sioux Falls in 1953.

Chapter 8
CULTURE AND RECREATION

CULTURE AND RECREATION

LITERATURE

South Dakota's literary heritage goes back to the early Sioux, who were superb storytellers. Elders passed their tribes' history down from one generation to the next in the form of legends. Some time after the arrival of white settlers and missionaries, a phonetic system was devised for writing the Sioux language. This allowed some of their legends to be written down for the first time. Today, many Sioux legends and stories have been translated into English.

Explorers, soldiers, and visitors from Europe were the first to write about the South Dakota region. They recorded all aspects of their journeys—the land, the wondrous buffalo herds, and encounters with Indian tribes. These journals provided the early settlers with information about the region.

The first real history of the Dakota Territory was written by Moses K. Armstrong in 1866. After that, several histories, atlases, and guides for immigrants were published. These books promoted the South Dakota region and encouraged more people to move there. Some of those pioneers eventually wrote their own impressions of life on South Dakota's prairie and became well-known authors.

Hamlin Garland, born in 1860 in Wisconsin, wrote about the struggles of pioneer life in the Aberdeen area. *Main-Travelled Roads, A Son of the Middle Border*, and *A Daughter of the Middle*

Border, for which he won a Pulitzer Prize in 1922, recount his experiences as the son of a Brown County homesteader.

New York native L. Frank Baum came to Aberdeen as a young man in the 1880s. There he edited and contributed humorous columns to the *Dakota Pioneer*, a weekly newspaper. When the paper went bankrupt, he moved to Chicago, where, in 1890, he wrote his well-loved *Wonderful Wizard of Oz*. Although the story is set against a cyclone in Kansas, some people think that his descriptions of the prairie and of the storm are based on his experiences in South Dakota.

Many novels set in South Dakota appeared during the early 1900s. Stewart Edward White, who lived in the Black Hills, used the mining town of Keystone for the setting of *The Westerners* and *The Claim Jumpers*—both published in 1901. In 1906, Sioux Falls dentist Will O. Lillibridge published *Ben Blair: The Story of a Plainsman*. This best-selling novel, about a young man growing up on a South Dakota cattle ranch, was later made into a movie.

In 1896, Ole Edvart Rölvaag came from Norway to work on his uncle's Elk Point farm. His famous novel *Giants in the Earth*, published in Norwegian in 1924 and in English in 1927, is set in the southeastern part of the state near Colton. It chronicles the hardships faced by Norwegian farmers living on the frontier.

Laura Ingalls, born in Wisconsin in 1867, moved to De Smet with her family in the late 1870s. In 1884, she married Almanzo Wilder; their daughter Rose was born in 1886; and in 1894, the Wilders left South Dakota for Missouri. Not until the late 1920s, however, did Laura Ingalls Wilder begin writing her ever-popular "Little House" books. De Smet, the town of *Little Town on the Prairie*, also provides the setting for four more of the nine "Little House" books: *By the Shores of Silver Lake*, *The Long Winter*, *These Happy Golden Years*, and *The First Four Years*. *The Long Winter*

In *The Long Winter*, Laura Ingalls Wilder depicted how the people of De Smet survived the horrible winter of 1880-81. This illustration from the book shows Laura's father attempting to save the family cattle.

describes the blizzards and near-starvation conditions suffered by the people of De Smet in 1880-81. Laura's daughter, Rose Wilder Lane, made De Smet the setting for two of her novels, *Let the Hurricane Roar* and *Free Land*.

Vine Deloria, Jr., a Yankton Sioux Episcopalian minister, is South Dakota's best-known contemporary writer. He has written several histories of the Sioux, including *Custer Died for Your Sins*, *God Is Red*, and *Behind the Trail of Broken Treaties*. These books describe the Sioux heritage and how white civilization and United States government policies have eroded the traditions and rights of many Sioux.

South Dakota has produced many poets. Charles Badger Clark, a Black Hills native, served as South Dakota's poet laureate from 1937 until his death in 1957. His many poems, of which "A Cowboy's Prayer," "The Job," and "The Glory Trail" are best known, celebrated life in the Black Hills and on the open range.

Kathleen Norris's poems reflect her love for her native state. After moving East, Norris returned to South Dakota in 1974 and settled in Lemmon, where she had spent childhood summers with her grandparents.

THE PERFORMING ARTS

Community and summer theaters thrive throughout the state. The drama departments of the state's colleges and universities regularly produce works that the public may attend. The Black Hills Passion Play, South Dakota's most famous production, is performed three times a week every summer in an outdoor amphitheater in Spearfish. Telling the story of the last week of the life of Jesus Christ, the play has been performed there since 1939.

The Black Hills Playhouse, in Custer State Park, began its first summer season in 1946. Associated with the College of Fine Arts of the University of South Dakota, the playhouse provides training for drama students from all over the nation. Dramas, musicals, and comedies entertain large audiences each summer.

South Dakotans and visitors alike attend opera and symphony productions. Guest opera performers present programs in Sioux Falls with the South Dakota Symphony Orchestra. Sioux Falls is also the home of the Sioux Empire Youth Symphony Orchestra, while Rapid City hosts the Black Hills Symphony Orchestra.

Country-and-western music is popular in South Dakota. It fills the air at the Mountain Music Show in Custer, the State Fair in Huron, many county fairs, and the South Dakota and Open Fiddling Contest in Yankton. Traditional Sioux music is performed at powwows throughout the summer in many reservation and Black Hills locations, including Custer, Fort Sisseton, and the Rosebud and Pine Ridge reservations.

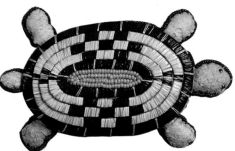

Some examples of traditional Sioux artwork

ART

South Dakota's first artists were Native Americans. With line drawings, they depicted historical events on sandstone outcroppings. Later, the Sioux used natural dyes to paint pictures on tepees, saddle blankets, and clothing. Some modern Sioux artisans use brightly colored geometric designs to adorn quilts, pottery, and intricate beadwork. Others create oil paintings using spiritual and cultural symbolism. Some of the pieces are used in ceremonies, while other items provide an income for the artists.

During the 1830s, artists such as George Catlin and Swiss-born Karl Bodmer traveled up the Missouri River to Fort Pierre. Their sketches and paintings of scenery and Indian life brought the Dakota area to life for people back east and in Europe. In 1843, John Audubon made a trip up the Missouri to complete his drawings of four-legged North American animals.

An 1832 painting by George Catlin of Steep Wind, a distinguished Sioux warrior

In the twentieth century, South Dakota produced two nationally respected artists: Harvey Dunn and Oscar Howe. Born on a Kingsbury County homestead near De Smet in 1884, Dunn reflected his love of the land in paintings of prairie and farm life. *The Harvest Orator* and *The Prairie is My Garden*, along with thirty-six other paintings, hang in the South Dakota Memorial Art Center at South Dakota State University in Brookings.

Oscar Howe, a Yanktonai Sioux born on the Crow Creek Indian Reservation in 1915, endured years of hardship before the art world recognized his paintings. Using traditional Sioux symbols, Howe expressed his people's values and religious beliefs in portraits and in paintings of Sioux ceremonies and dances.

In 1943, as part of a WPA project, Howe designed and painted

Sioux Seed Player, **by noted South Dakota artist Oscar Howe**

Sun and Rain Clouds Over the Hills in the rotunda of what is now the Oscar Howe Art Center in Mitchell. The center also displays more than twenty of his paintings. Fine examples of his work can also be seen at the Oscar Howe Gallery at the University of South Dakota in Vermillion. Howe was a professor and artist-in-residence at the university from 1957 until his death in 1983. During that time, he was named artist laureate of South Dakota. Between 1948 and 1971, Howe designed the annually changing mosaics—composed of different-colored ears of corn and other grains—that decorate the exterior of the Corn Palace in Mitchell. This unusual South Dakota landmark is the site of a famous annual harvest festival. Six of Howe's panels are part of a permanent indoor exhibit at the palace.

Two well-known American sculptors did their most famous

Left: A model of the Crazy Horse
Memorial juxtaposed against the
actual, still-unfinished monument
Above: Korczak Ziolkowski

work in the granite mountains of the Black Hills. In 1927, Gutzon
Borglum started drilling, blasting, and carving the heads of
American Presidents George Washington, Thomas Jefferson,
Abraham Lincoln, and Theodore Roosevelt into Mount Rushmore.
After Borglum died, in 1941, his son Lincoln directed the project.
Seven months later, however, work was halted on the almost-
completed national memorial. Because of World War II, Congress
could no longer appropriate funds for its completion.

Six years after work halted on Mount Rushmore—and 17 miles
(27 kilometers) to the southwest—Korczak Ziolkowski began
work on the Crazy Horse Memorial at Thunderhead Mountain.
Carving an image of Crazy Horse, on his horse, out of the granite
mountain became Ziolkowski's lifework. This 563-foot-
(172-meter-) high by 641-foot- (195-meter-) long memorial—the
largest sculptural undertaking the world has ever known—is far
from completion. Forty-three years later and eight years after his

The annual Balloon Rally in Sioux Falls

death, Ziolkowski's family continues to direct the work on the sculpture.

Dale Lamphere, a sculptor from Sturgis, has completed four bronze statues for the rotunda of the South Dakota State Capitol. These statues represent human qualities important in the development of South Dakota: wisdom, vision, courage, and integrity.

FAIRS AND FESTIVALS

On almost any weekend of the year, some community in South Dakota is hosting a fair, festival, or rodeo. South Dakotans enjoy celebrating their history, their ethnic and agricultural backgrounds, and the seasons.

Aberdeen starts off each year with the Snow Queen Festival in January. A hot-air balloon rally and antique-car show highlight Sturgis's annual Spring Festival, held on Mother's Day weekend.

Brookings's Summer Festival attracts artists and craftspeople from around the nation. Indian dances, muzzle-loading demonstrations, craft exhibits, and dramatic and music programs round out Custer's Fall Festival each September.

Throughout the summer months, many towns celebrate their frontier history. Fort Sisseton Historical Festival at Fort Sisseton State Park features displays of frontier crafts and demonstrations of cavalry and infantry skills. The Laura Ingalls Wilder Pageant near De Smet is a dramatization of *The Long Winter*. Logging events are featured at Black Hills Sawdust Day in Spearfish and at Heart of the Hills Celebration in Hill City. The gold-rush days are celebrated during Deadwood's Days of '76 and Custer's Gold Discovery Days.

Schmeckfest is a food-tasting fair sponsored each April by Freeman's Hutterite community. In June, Czechs celebrate their heritage in Tabor, and Scandinavians hold heritage days at Augustana College in Sioux Falls. Each August, the Rosebud Sioux Tribal Affairs and Powwow features traditional dances, arts, crafts, and a buffalo dinner.

Agricultural exhibits are the main attractions at the county fairs held throughout the state and, of course, at the State Fair held in Huron. Other events that highlight agriculture include the Little International in Brookings and the Sioux Empire Farm Show in Sioux Falls. Every September, Mitchell hosts the Corn Palace Festival to salute corn's important role in that part of the state.

In July and August, towns throughout the state put on rodeos featuring bull riding, bucking-bronco riding, and cow roping. Mobridge's Sitting Bull Stampede, the Black Hills Roundup in Belle Fourche, and the Corn Palace Stampede in Mitchell are a few of South Dakota's rodeos. August is also a month for water festivals. Pierre celebrates Oahe Days at Oahe Dam with a raft race and a buffalo chip flip. Boating and waterskiing contests highlight Yankton's Riverboat Days. Another famous August event is the Sturgis Motorcycle Rally. In 1990, more than 300,000 cyclists celebrated the fiftieth anniversary of the event.

SPORTS AND RECREATION

South Dakotans and visitors alike enjoy the state's lakes. The Great Lakes of South Dakota—Oahe, Sharpe, Francis Case, and Lewis and Clark—the glacial lakes of the northeast, and many others have facilities for camping, swimming, fishing, and boating. More than five hundred lakes and nearly a hundred rivers provide enthusiastic anglers with a variety of fish.

Skiing and snowmobiling are other popular winter sports. Terry Peak and Deer Mountain, both in the Lead-Deadwood area, and Great Bear, near Sioux Falls, provide miles of ski runs. Six lifts at Terry Peak can bring 5,500 skiers up to the runs per hour. Cross-country ski trails are found at all three downhill ski areas, in nineteen of the state's parks and recreation areas, and in the Black Hills National Forest. Close to 450 miles (724 kilometers) of snowmobile trails wind through the Black Hills and the eastern lake region. Snowmobilers may also use more than 1 million acres (404,690 hectares) of public land.

South Dakota provides unlimited opportunities for horseback riders, hikers, climbers, and rock hounds. Horseback riders and hikers enjoy miles of marked trails in the many state parks. Hikers are challenged to follow the Centennial Trail, which runs 111 miles (179 kilometers) from Bear Butte State Park through Custer State Park to Wind Cave National Park. Rock hounds collect a variety of rocks, fossils, minerals, and gemstones, including crystals, agates, petrified wood, alabaster, and gypsum.

Hikers in Badlands National Park

South Dakota is a hunter's paradise. Hunting licenses are required, and the hunting season for each kind of game is defined by law. Ring-necked pheasants, sharp-tailed grouse, mourning doves, gray partridges, prairie chickens, mallard ducks, and Canada, blue, and snow geese are hunted in various parts of the state. Hunting of deer and pronghorn antelope is also permitted.

Although the state has no major-league sports teams, it has two professional basketball teams, and South Dakotans avidly follow their favorite high school and college teams. Most of the colleges and universities field teams in football, basketball, and baseball, as well as other sports. Other spectator sports include horse racing in Aberdeen, Fort Pierre, and Rapid City; greyhound racing in Rapid City; and stock-car racing and rodeoing throughout the state.

Chapter 9
TOURING THE SUNSHINE STATE

TOURING THE SUNSHINE STATE

From the glacial lakes in the northeast to the Black Hills and Badlands in the southwest, the Sunshine State's natural wonders give pleasure to South Dakotans and attract tourists from around the world. The industries and museums of South Dakota's cities and towns hold many surprises for travelers. The following six brief tours of the state highlight some of its best-known attractions.

GLACIAL LAKES REGION

Eight state parks, eight state recreation areas, and one state nature area are located in the glacial lakes region of northeastern South Dakota. Bird-watchers flock to Big Stone Island Nature Area in Big Stone Lake, which can be reached only by boat. Glacial lakes also provide the setting for Hartford Beach State Park on Big Stone Lake, Roy Lake State Park, and Lake Poinsett Recreation Area.

Milbank, close to the South Dakota-Minnesota border south of Hartford Beach State Park, is the birthplace of American Legion baseball. Tours of the town's red mahogany granite quarries and the Old Windmill, a white-with-red-trim English gristmill, are available. West of Milbank, near Marvin, stands the contemporary-style Blue Cloud Abbey, built by Benedictine monks who work to further Indian education. The American Indian Cultural Center, which features Indian art, is located on the grounds. To the northwest is Fort Sisseton State Park.

Sunrise over one of the glacial lakes of northeastern South Dakota

Fourteen of the fort's brick and stone buildings have been restored and can be visited year-round. During the first weekend in June, volunteers demonstrate late nineteenth-century frontier crafts and military skills. In July, the Sisseton-Wahpeton Sioux hold their annual powwow at Old Agency near the town of Sisseton.

Aberdeen, the largest city in the glacial lakes region, serves as the area's business, trade, and transportation center. The art gallery at Northern State University (NSC) and theater productions and music concerts by NSC, Presentation College, and community groups provide a cultural life for the area. Dacotah Prairie Museum displays pioneer and Indian artifacts, clothing, and rooms furnished to represent various periods of the area's history.

The Shrine to Music Museum, in Vermillion, houses more than three thousand musical instruments and related musical memorabilia.

Directly south lies Huron, hometown of Hubert H. Humphrey. Once a contender for the site of the state's capital, Huron today hosts the Huron Air Show each June, the Meadowood Art Fair in August, and the State Fair in September. Humphrey Drugstore, owned by the vice-president and his family until his death in 1978, maintains a 1930s atmosphere. Carved woodwork and stained glass attract visitors to the Queen Anne-style Gladys Pyle Historic Home. Pyle was the first South Dakota woman elected to the United States Senate.

Due east is De Smet, the setting for Laura Ingalls Wilder's *Little Town on the Prairie* and other "Little House" books. A guided tour takes visitors through the restored surveyor's house that served as the Ingalls's home during the winter of 1879-80, Ma and Pa Ingalls's home, and other places mentioned in Wilder's books.

The town of Lake Norden, to the northeast, houses the world's only amateur Baseball Hall of Fame. Farther north is Watertown, located on the shores of Lakes Pelican and Kampeska. Mellette House, the home of South Dakota's last territorial governor and first state governor, Arthur C. Mellette, includes the home's original furniture, family portraits, and heirlooms.

To the south lies Brookings. Research done at South Dakota State University's Agricultural Experiment Station has made the city South Dakota's agricultural capital. The university, with its State Agricultural Heritage Museum and South Dakota Memorial Art Center, also plays a leading cultural role in Brookings.

Madison, at the southern tip of the glacial lakes region, is home to Dakota State University. Prairie Village, west of Madison, is a replica of an 1890s town. The village's attractions include fifty restored buildings, antique tractors, a steam-powered merry-go-round, and steam-train rides.

SOUTHEASTERN PIONEER CITIES

Southeastern South Dakota contains Sioux Falls, the state's largest city, as well as towns with the flavor of rural America. This region also provides outdoor adventure at four state recreation areas, three state parks, and two of the state's three nature areas.

Adams Nature Area, in the state's far southeast corner, preserves 628 acres (254 hectares) of Missouri River bottomland. Nature lovers can study waterfowl, wildlife, and plant life there. To the northwest, high on a bluff above the Vermillion River, sits the city of Vermillion. As is true in Brookings, much of Vermillion's life centers on its university—the University of South Dakota. Most of Vermillion's museums and art galleries are found on campus, including the Oscar Howe Gallery, the Warren M. Lee Center for the Fine Arts, and the Coyote Student Center. The Shrine to Music Museum houses more than three thousand

Sioux Falls at night

musical instruments, some of which date back to 3300 B.C. The
W. H. Over Museum exhibits artifacts relating to the state's
natural and cultural history.

Sioux Falls serves as the region's cultural, educational, and
medical center, as well as its transportation hub. With annual
retail sales exceeding $800 million, the city leads the state in
manufacturing and in agriculture-related and services-related
businesses. The John Morrell meat-packing plant and Citibank,
the credit card operation for Citicorp, the world's largest bank
holding company, are located in Sioux Falls.

There is much to see in Sioux Falls. The Great Plains Zoo in
Sherman Park has 6 acres (2.4 hectares) along the Big Sioux River
devoted to Great Plains grasses and animals such as prairie dogs,
coyotes, and mule deer. Other exhibits feature animals from
Africa and Asia. The Delbridge Museum of Natural History, also
in Sherman Park, houses one of the world's largest displays of

mounted animals from all over the world. The Pettigrew Home and Museum, built in 1889, depicts the life of South Dakota's first senator. It also includes items explaining the natural history and Native American history of the region.

Due west of Sioux Falls lies Mitchell, home of the world's only Corn Palace. This building's architectural style, with its Moorish minarets and turrets, is truly unique. An annual Corn Palace Festival is held there in the fall to honor the area's agricultural heritage. Each year, in preparation for the festival, more than three thousand bushels of corn and other grains are used to create the murals that adorn the Corn Palace's exterior. A few blocks west, the Oscar Howe Art Center showcases Howe's mural in the rotunda and several of his paintings, as well as works of other local artists.

The Prehistoric Indian Village, located north of town on Lake Mitchell, continues to provide clues for archaeologists about the people who lived on this site a thousand years ago. At the south end of town is the Friends of the Middle Border Museum of Pioneer Life. Included on the grounds is an 1885 one-room schoolhouse, a railroad depot, a general store, and the 1886 Beckwith House, home of a cofounder of the Corn Palace. The museum contains manuscripts of L. Frank Baum, Hamlin Garland, Rose Wilder Lane, and Ole Rölvaag, and artworks of Gutzon Borglum, Ada Caldwell, Harvey Dunn, and Oscar Howe.

THE GREAT LAKES REGION

South Dakota's "great lakes" region spans the Missouri River valley from the North Dakota border to the Nebraska border. Besides the state's four largest lakes, South Dakota's capital and parts of four Indian reservations are located in this region.

Lake Oahe extends from about 65 miles (105 kilometers) inside North Dakota to just north of Pierre. Its 2,250-mile (3,621-kilometer) shoreline provides endless hours of excitement for campers, boaters, anglers, swimmers, and water-skiers. To the north, on the western side of the lake, are the adjoining Standing Rock and Cheyenne River Indian reservations. On the Standing Rock Reservation, home of the Hunkpapa and Yanktonai Sioux, Sitting Bull's grave is marked by a bust sculpted by Korczak Ziolkowski. Nearby stands a monument honoring Sacajawea, the Shoshone Indian woman who guided Lewis and Clark along the Missouri River.

Mobridge, located on the eastern shore of Lake Oahe, is the largest town in this northern area. Although famous for its walleye, northern pike, and salmon fishing, Mobridge's economy is based on outlying farms and ranches. In town, the Klein Museum displays pioneer antiques and Arikara and Sioux artifacts. Oscar Howe's ten colorful murals illustrating Sioux history and ceremonies decorate the walls of the Mobridge Municipal Auditorium.

Hoven, to the southeast, is proud of its "Cathedral on the Prairie." St. Anthony Catholic Church is a small-scale copy of a thousand-year-old church in Ruhmannsfelden, Germany. Bavarian stained-glass windows and huge arches and columns trimmed in gold leaf decorate this lovely South Dakota prairie church.

Pierre, located in the center of the state, is South Dakota's capital city. South Dakota granite boulders provide the foundation for the Greek-style state capitol. Near the capitol, the Cultural Heritage Center displays Indian, pioneer, and mining exhibits. On the shores of Capitol Lake, visitors admire the Flaming Fountain Veterans Memorial, with its continually burning flame. Across the

The Dakota Territorial Museum in Yankton includes the restored Dakota Territorial Legislative Council Building.

river, at Fort Pierre, the Vérendrye Monument marks the site where, in 1743, the La Vérendrye brothers buried a lead plate to bolster France's claim to the Louisiana region.

To the south is Lake Sharpe, famous for its year-round walleye fishing. Surrounding the lake are the Crow Creek and Lower Brûlé Indian reservations. The southern portions of these reservations adjoin Lake Francis Case. Sightseers can reach Big Bend Dam and Powerhouse from either reservation and can visit frontier-era Forts Defiance, Hale, and Kiowa on the Lower Brûlé Reservation.

Chamberlain and tiny Oacoma, located on opposite sides of the northern end of Lake Francis Case, afford a magnificent view of the Missouri River Valley. For many years, ferries transported passengers and freight to the western bank of the Missouri. Today, travelers experience the awe of the pioneers as they cross the wide Missouri via the Interstate 90 bridge.

Following the Missouri River as it curves to the east, visitors arrive in the Lewis and Clark Recreation Area. Its year-round outdoor fun centers around Lewis and Clark Lake. Skating, ice fishing, and iceboating on the lake in winter provide special enjoyment. Gavins Point Dam, which formed the lake, is located on the site where Lewis and Clark exchanged gifts and ate with about seventy Sioux in 1804. Below the dam, anglers still catch or snare paddlefish, a survivor from prehistoric times found only in the Missouri River and in China's Yangtze River.

A few miles east of Gavins Point Dam is Yankton, the largest and southernmost city of the great lakes region. Yankton's years as the first capital of the Dakota Territory are remembered in its restored homes and mansions. The Dakota Territory Museum is a complex that houses the restored Dakota Territorial Legislative Council Building.

THE BADLANDS AND SURROUNDING AREA

Each summer, the population temporarily swells as over a million people enter the Badlands to enjoy its natural wonders and historic attractions.

Murdo, on the eastern edge of the region, stands on the trail of the old cattle drives from Texas. The dividing line between central time and mountain time goes through the town. The cattle business still remains important to the town's economy. Murdo's main attraction is the Pioneer Auto Museum and Antique Town, which has more than two hundred cars, some dating to 1902, and a reconstructed town with thirty-seven buildings.

South of Murdo, on the Nebraska border, are three towns on the Rosebud Indian Reservation, home to the Brûlé Sioux. Mission serves as the reservation's trading center. Rosebud is the tribal

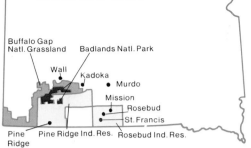

A cookout during a powwow on the Rosebud Indian Reservation

and federal administrative center and the site of Sinte Gleska College and the annual Rosebud Fair and Powwow. St. Francis is a cultural center. Its Buechel Memorial Lakota Museum features beautiful exhibits of Sioux arts and crafts.

The 120,000-acre (48,563 hectare) Pine Ridge Reservation touches the Rosebud Reservation's northwest corner. The second-largest reservation in the nation, Pine Ridge is home to the Oglala Sioux. The Red Cloud Indian Mission, near the town of Pine Ridge, runs an elementary and a secondary school, sells Native American crafts, and hosts an Indian art show each summer.

Northeast of Pine Ridge is the Wounded Knee Battlefield, which commemorates the December 1890 massacre by the United States army that left more than two hundred Sioux men, women, and children dead. Oglala Lakota College and a large part of Badlands National Park are also on the reservation.

Towering granite spires are part of the landscape of the Black Hills.

Kadoka, north of the eastern edge of the reservation, serves as the eastern gateway to the Badlands. Meaning "hole-in-the-wall" in Sioux, Kadoka is an opening in the rim of the Badlands' wall. Hikers and campers stock up on supplies there in preparation for their adventure into the rugged Badlands.

Before entering Badlands National Park, near Cactus Flat, visitors stop to view the Prairie Homestead, built in 1909 by the Brown family. Cut into the side of a hill, the home had a dirt roof, buffalo-grass sod wall, and cottonwood-log front. Equipped as it was when the Brown family lived there, the homestead is a vivid reminder of the harsh living conditions that the pioneers were willing to endure.

South of the homestead is the entrance to Badlands National Park, named a national monument in 1929 and a national park ten years later. In the northern part of the park, from Cactus Flat to Wall, a 32-mile (51 kilometer) loop road cuts through the park's 243,302 acres (98,462 hectares). Along this most-traveled route in the park are overlooks from which visitors may view stunning formations that were formed over millions of years by wind and water erosion. More adventurous travelers climb or walk out into the unusual rock formations. Cedar Pass Visitor Center offers natural-history displays and a "touch room" where visitors can put on a buffalo robe, hold deer antlers, and examine fossils.

At the western end of the loop road, where it rejoins Interstate 90, is the town of Wall. During the tourist season, about ten thousand people a day stop for a free glass of ice water at the world-famous Wall Drug Store. Although drugstores had been offering free ice water for years, the Husteads, who bought the store in 1931, began *advertising* free ice water in 1936. Today, Wall Drug is an extensive shopping center with specialty shops; art galleries; a chapel; and a 520-seat restaurant featuring buffalo burgers and five-cent cups of coffee.

As travelers leave the Badlands, they cross through the Buffalo Gap National Grassland. This protected area, which has many private cattle ranches, borders the Badlands to the north and west.

THE BLACK HILLS

Rapid City, the gateway to the Black Hills, also serves as the area's commercial, industrial, and cultural center. Founded two years after the discovery of gold in the Black Hills, Rapid City — today the state's second-largest city — is still a place where mining-related industries remain important. Tourism, lumbering, and agriculture are also important aspects of the city's economy. Shrewd shoppers can buy Black Hills gold jewelry and western leather goods at bargain prices.

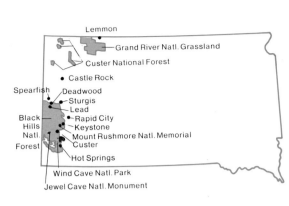

The Mammoth Site near Hot Springs

Rapid City also offers many museums and cultural events. Rushmore Plaza Civic Center headlines concerts, plays, art exhibits, trade shows, professional basketball, state high-school athletic tournaments, and the annual Black Hills and Northern Plains Indian Powwow. In Halley Park, the Sioux Indian Museum and Craft Center traces the region's history through Indian arts and crafts, and nearby Minnelusa Pioneer Museum displays tools and supplies of the early settlers. South Dakota School of Mines and Technology's Museum of Geology highlights fossils from the Badlands and dinosaur bones found in the northwestern part of the state.

Northeast of Rapid City is Ellsworth Air Force Base and the South Dakota Air and Space Museum. Southwest of the city stands the Chapel in the Hills, an exact replica of an 800-year-old Norwegian wooden church with intricate carvings.

Highways from Rapid City lead to the towns and attractions in the Black Hills National Forest, which also extends into Wyoming.

Wind Cave National Park

A warm-water river flows through the southern Black Hills town of Hot Springs. Indians thought the waters had curative powers, and today residents and visitors collect bottles of mineral water daily. Evans Plunge, the world's largest natural warm-water, indoor swimming pool, attracts swimmers all year. Also located in Hot Springs is the Mammoth Site, where diggers continue to uncover the bones of prehistoric animals that became trapped in a sinkhole more than twenty-six thousand years ago.

Wind Cave National Park, to the north, provides a home for pronghorn antelope, prairie dogs, mule deer, coyotes, elk, and a herd of buffalo. Wind Cave, discovered in 1881, got its name from a change in atmospheric pressure that caused a strong wind to blow through the cave. Today, spelunkers can explore more than 30 miles (48 kilometers) of passageways decorated with boxwork and frostwork limestone formations.

The Black Hills have more crystal caves than any other place in the world. Northwest of Wind Cave, Jewel Cave National Monument is the world's fourth-longest cave system, with over 70 miles (113 kilometers) of passageways. Calcite crystal formations, sparkling like jewels, gave the cave its name.

East of Jewel Cave lies the town of Custer, where gold was discovered in 1874 by General Custer's men. Each evening, the town's Mountain Music Show features country music and comedy. North of town, atop Thunderhead Mountain, Korczak Ziolkowski's family continues to work on his carving of Chief Crazy Horse. Visitors to the memorial can view the scale model of the finished sculpture and tour Ziolkowski's eighty-two-room log-cabin home and studio.

East of Custer sprawls 73,000-acre (29,542-hectare) Custer State Park. At the southern end of the park, travelers on the Wildlife Loop Road may observe pronghorn antelope and some of the park's fourteen hundred buffalo. South of Center Lake, the Black Hills Playhouse produces well-known dramas, comedies, and musicals during the summer season. Named for the tall, pointed granite formations along its route, Needles Highway provides spectacular views of Harney Peak on its way northwest to Sylvan Lake. Iron Mountain road leads out of the park to Keystone and Mount Rushmore National Memorial. The road's many tunnels were blasted to provide views of Gutzon Borglum's world-famous mountain sculpture.

In Keystone, which was a busy gold-mining town in the 1880s, visitors may pan for gold and take a guided underground tour through Big Thunder Gold Mine. Men who came to work on the national memorial made their homes in Keystone. Today, the town's economy focuses on tourists on their way to Mount Rushmore. The Rushmore-Borglum Story and Gallery preserves

Visitors to Mount Rushmore (left) can also tour Gutzon Borglum's studio (right).

the furniture and tools used in Borglum's South Dakota studio and displays a large collection of his paintings and statues. Visitors can take helicopter rides or an aerial tramway from Keystone to view Mount Rushmore. At the memorial itself, the 60-foot- (18-meter-) high faces of Presidents Washington, Jefferson, Lincoln, and Theodore Roosevelt attract more than 2 million visitors each year.

In the northern Black Hills are the towns of Lead, Deadwood, Sturgis, Spearfish, and Belle Fourche. Lead, South Dakota's mile-high city, is best known as the site of the Homestake Gold Mine, the largest gold-producing mine in the Western Hemisphere. The mine has a large "open cut," as well as numerous underground tunnels. Summer visitors can take a tour of the surface workings of the mine and learn about gold production. The Sinking Gardens, a city park, got its name when the ground started to sink

Highlights of Deadwood include the No. 10 Saloon (left) and Mount Moriah Cemetery (right).

because of the many gold mine tunnels under it. Winter visitors enjoy skiing at nearby Terry Peak and Deer Mountain.

Located in a gulch a few miles north, Deadwood, with its one main street, saw about thirty thousand gold rushers build a tent town almost overnight in 1876. Today a national historic site, the town attracts crowds of tourists with its Wild West heritage. The No. 10 Saloon marks the spot where Jack McCall shot Wild Bill Hickok. Each day, the entire event, from the shooting to McCall's trial, is reenacted. A short walk up a steep hill leads to the graves of Wild Bill, Calamity Jane, and Preacher Smith in Mount Moriah Cemetery. The Chinese Tunnel Tour explains the role of Deadwood's Chinese settlers during the gold rush. At the edge of town, Broken Boot Gold Mine offers demonstrations of gold mining.

Sturgis, north of Deadwood, began as a wagon stop on the way to Fort Meade. Now a busy trading center for the Black Hills, Sturgis remembers its past through preserving the homes of Annie Tallent and "Poker Alice" Tubbs. Tallent, the first pioneer woman in the Black Hills, wrote a history of the area in 1898. In contrast, Tubbs, queen of the women gamblers, ran a rowdy saloon.

East of town is the Old Fort Meade and Cavalry Museum, erected in 1878 to keep the peace between settlers and the Indians. North of Sturgis stands Bear Butte. The Sioux, who considered it sacred, named it *Matȯ Pahȧ*, "Sleeping Bear Mountain." Both the Sioux and Cheyenne continue to hold religious ceremonies there.

West of Sturgis and north of scenic Spearfish Canyon lies Spearfish. Known for its famed Black Hills Passion Play, the town also produces melodramas, based on local Wild West legends, at the Matthews Opera House. The Berry Library at Black Hills State University houses Lyndle Dunn's wildlife art, Babylonian tablets, and porcelain miniatures depicting the nation's first ladies. Farthest north in the Black Hills is the town of Belle Fourche. Once the site of a range war between cattle and sheep ranchers, the town remains the nation's wool-shipping center. Mining and milling of bentonite are other important industries in Belle Fourche. Sightseers enjoy visiting the restored, 1876 two-story cabin built by Johnny Spaulding, a pioneer Indian scout. The Black Hills Roundup, which includes a professional rodeo, is a major summer attraction.

THE NORTHWESTERN REGION

Northwestern South Dakota is the least-populated part of the state; towns and people are few and far between. Located a few miles west of Castle Rock is the geographical center of the United

The Petrified Wood Park in Lemmon

States. Forests, grasslands, and several buttes, which jut up on the landscape, break up this rugged, hilly region.

Custer National Forest covers 73,489 acres (29,740 hectares) of the northwest corner of the area. The forest's Slim Buttes area looks like a forested Badlands, with its pine-topped hills and limestone cliffs. Despite the rugged land, campers, hikers, and hunters who like "roughing it" enjoy the area's natural beauty. To the east stretch thousands of acres of Grand River National Grassland. Some of this land is leased by sheep ranchers.

Lemmon, located on the North Dakota border, is the region's largest town, with 1,871 people. Founded by George E. Lemmon, pioneer cowboy and member of the National Cowboy Hall of Fame, the town serves as the trading center for this part of North and South Dakota. Visitors stand in awe of gigantic petrified wood logs—up to 10 feet (3 meters) in diameter—at the Petrified Wood Park. Indoor and outdoor displays of 200-million-year-old fossils are also featured. South of town, Llewellyn John's Recreation Area has many buildings made of petrified wood.

Parts of Custer National Forest, in the northwest part of the state, resemble a forested Badlands.

Canoeists and bass and pike fishers use nearby Flat Creek Lake. Rock hounds hunt for glasslike calcite crystals at Shadehill Recreation Area. Close to Shadehill stands the Hugh Glass Monument. Glass was a hunter and guide for a trading party in 1823. Mauled by a grizzly bear, he was left for dead by the rest of the party. Weeks later and with great determination, Glass reached Fort Kiowa, the present-day site of Chamberlain.

South Dakota's rugged northwest ends the tour of the Sunshine State. Taking pride in their heritage, South Dakotans remain honest, hardworking people who continue to develop their farms, ranches, cities, and industries and to preserve the state's natural resources and environment. After enjoying the state's many natural wonders and touring its unique towns and cities, visitors agree that South Dakota is the Land of Infinite Variety.

FACTS AT A GLANCE

GENERAL INFORMATION

Statehood: November 2, 1889, fortieth state

Origin of Name: North Dakota and South Dakota were named for the Sioux Indians, who called themselves "Dakota," meaning "allies."

State Capital: Pierre, since 1890

State Nicknames: Sunshine State, Coyote State, Land of Infinite Variety

State Flag: South Dakota's state flag bears the state seal on a sky-blue background. Above the seal, in gold letters, is "South Dakota"; below the seal is "The Sunshine State." Gold rays representing the sun surround the seal. A farmer planting a field of corn symbolizes agriculture. Cattle feeding on the plain represent ranching and dairying. A smelting furnace depicts the state's mining industry. A riverboat moving along the Missouri River stands for transportation and commerce. The seal also contains the words "State of South Dakota" and "Great 1889 Seal," the year the state entered the Union.

State Motto: "Under God the People Rule"

State Flower: American pasqueflower

State Bird: Chinese ring-necked pheasant

State Grass: Western wheat grass

State Tree: Black Hills spruce

State Insect: Honeybee

State Animal: Coyote

State Mineral: Rose quartz

State Gemstone: Fairburn agate

State Colors: Blue and gold

State Fish: Walleye

State Song: "Hail, South Dakota," words and music by Deecort Hammitt, adopted as the state song in 1943:

Hail! South Dakota,
A great state of the land,
Health, wealth, and beauty,
That's what makes her grand;
She has her Black Hills,
And mines with gold so rare,
And with her scen'ry,
No state can compare.

POPULATION

Population: 696,004, forty-fifth among the states (1990 census)

Population Density: 9 persons per sq. mi. (3.5 persons per km²)

Population Distribution: Less than half of South Dakota's population live in cities and towns. Sioux Falls, near the eastern boundary with Iowa and Minnesota, is South Dakota's largest city.

Sioux Falls	100,814
Rapid City	54,523
Aberdeen	24,927
Watertown	17,592
Brookings	16,270
Mitchell	13,798
Pierre	12,906
Yankton	12,703
Huron	12,448
Vermillion	10,034

(Population figures according to 1990 census)

Population Growth: Few states have shown smaller population growth over the years than South Dakota. Its population jumped rapidly in the years before statehood, but tapered off after 1910. The state has begun to see a population increase again since 1980. Only in recent years has South Dakota exceeded its 1930 population peak of 692,849. After 1930, many people left the state because of hard times caused by the Great Depression and drought.

Year	Population
1860	4,837
1880	98,268
1900	401,570
1920	636,547
1930	692,849
1940	642,961
1950	652,740
1960	680,514
1970	666,257
1980	690,768
1990	696,004

GEOGRAPHY

Borders: South Dakota is bordered by North Dakota on the north, Minnesota and Iowa on the east, Nebraska on the south, and Wyoming and Montana on the west.

Highest Point: Harney Peak, in Pennington County, 7,242 ft. (2,207 m)

Lowest Point: Big Stone Lake, in Roberts County, 962 ft. (293 m)

Greatest Distances: North to south—237 mi. (381 km)
East to west—383 mi. (616 km)

Area: 77,116 sq. mi. (199,730 km²)

Rank in Area Among the States: Sixteenth

National Forests and Parklands: Some of America's most storied national lands are found in western South Dakota. South Dakota shares its two national forests with other states. Black Hills National Forest spreads into Wyoming, and part of Custer National Forest lies in Montana.
In South Dakota's famed Badlands region is Badlands National Park, a barren region of bizarre and beautiful rock landscapes. Mount Rushmore National Memorial, the state's most famous tourist attraction, features the faces of four American presidents sculpted into the side of a Black Hills mountain. Also in the Black Hills area are Jewel Cave National Monument, which contains calcite crystals that shine and sparkle like jewels; and Wind Cave National Park, named for the strong winds that blow through its limestone caverns. Three national grasslands— Buffalo Gap, Fort Pierre, and Grand River—cover parts of western South Dakota.

Rivers: The Missouri River, the longest river in North America, flows from north to south through the heart of the state. The Missouri and its tributaries drain

A thunderstorm in central South Dakota

virtually the entire state. The Grand, Bad, Moreau, Cheyenne, and White rivers are the largest tributaries passing through the western portion of the state. The James, Big Sioux, and Vermillion rivers are the largest tributaries in eastern South Dakota. Rivers in the northeast flow into Lake Traverse or Big Stone Lake.

Lakes: South Dakota contains more than 250 natural lakes, most of them northeastern lakes formed by the action of glaciers. Big Stone Lake and Lake Traverse are the two largest such lakes. The state also contains hundreds of man-made bodies of water. These range from small farm ponds to the huge lakes along the Missouri River—Lakes Oahe, Sharpe, Francis Case, and Lewis and Clark— known as the "Great Lakes of South Dakota." These four lakes were formed by building four dams along the Missouri: Oahe Dam, Gavins Point Dam, Big Bend Dam, and Fort Randall Dam.

Topography: From east to west, South Dakota moves from gentle hills, to plains and prairies, to eroded yet rugged mountains. An area known as the Dissected Till Plains cuts into southeastern South Dakota. Rich soil left by retreating glaciers is cut by rivers passing through the area. The Drift Prairie covers the rest of eastern South Dakota. This region contains glacial lakes and low, rolling hills.

A steep slope near the James River separates the Drift Prairie from the Great Plains. This region, covering most of the western two-thirds of South Dakota,

112

includes rolling hills and plains, as well as the rugged terrain of the Badlands, with its sharp peaks and deep gullies cut by wind and water. In the far western part of South Dakota rise the Black Hills. This mineral-rich range of domed mountains is an eastern extension of the Rocky Mountains.

Climate: South Dakota's settlers had to be hardy to withstand the fierce climate they encountered. Blistering heat could occur in the summertime. Blizzards often proved deadly in winter. Spring flooding could destroy homes and freshly planted crops. Tornadoes always loomed as a summer threat. Rainfall was uncertain, and drought could spoil a harvest. Yet the weather could also be beautiful.

Temperatures in Sioux Falls, in the southeastern part of the state, range from 24° F. to 4° F. (-4° C to -16° C) in January and from 88° F. to 62° F. (31° C to 17° C) in July. Rapid City, in the Black Hills, experiences temperatures ranging from 33° F. to 9° F. (1° C to -13° C) in January and from 86° F. to 59° F. (30° C to 15° C) in July. Precipitation ranges from about 13 in. (33 cm) in the northeast to 25 in. (64 cm) in the southeast.

NATURE

Trees: Oaks, maples, cottonwoods, junipers, spruces, beeches, birches, willows, ashes, pines, elms

Wild Plants: Wild plums, gooseberries, currants, pasqueflowers, beardtongues, bluebells, black-eyed Susans, goldenrod, mariposa lilies, poppies, sunflowers, cacti, forget-me-nots, blazing stars, lady's-slippers, larkspurs, chokecherry, yucca

Animals: Coyotes, porcupines, brown snakes, rattlesnakes, ferrets, Blandings turtles, pronghorn antelopes, buffalo, bobcats, white-tailed deer, mule deer, jackrabbits, prairie dogs, river otters, mountain lions, northern swift foxes, black bears, squirrels, badgers, gophers

Birds: Sage grouse, prairie chickens, bobwhite quail, ring-necked pheasant, peregrine falcons, wild turkeys, Hungarian partridges, red-winged blackbirds, yellow-headed blackbirds, crossbills, rock wrens, eagles

Fish: Rainbow trout, brown trout, brook trout, catfish, northern pike, walleye, chinook salmon, bass, perch, longnose suckers, crappies, sturgeon, saugers

GOVERNMENT

South Dakota still uses its first constitution, adopted in 1889. However, the document has been amended more than eighty times.

Like the federal government, South Dakota's government is divided into three branches. The legislative (law-making) branch consists of a 70-member house of representatives and a 35-member senate. The state's voters elect a senator and two representatives from each of 35 districts. Members of both houses serve two-year terms. South Dakota's initiative and referendum processes allow voters a major say in state government. Initiative allows voters to pass laws directly if they obtain enough petition signatures to get a suggested law on the ballot. Through referendum, 5 percent of the voters can request a vote by the people to reject laws passed by the legislature.

The governor heads the executive branch, which also includes the lieutenant governor, secretary of state, attorney general, treasurer, auditor, and commissioner of school and public lands. All serve four-year terms. The governor and lieutenant governor may serve only two consecutive terms. Other officials may serve an unlimited number of terms.

The judicial branch consists of the state's court system. The state supreme court is the highest court in South Dakota. Its judges are elected to eight-year terms. The judges elect their own chief justice. Below the supreme court is the circuit court, which has 36 judges in eight judicial districts. Nineteen county court districts and municipal courts in Sioux Falls, Rapid City, and Aberdeen are also part of the judicial system. The judges in all of these courts are elected.

Number of Counties: 66

U.S. Representatives: 1

Electoral Votes: 3

Voting Qualifications: Eighteen years of age, registered to vote fifteen days before election

EDUCATION

Even while they were struggling to earn a living for themselves, early South Dakotans cared about their children's education. The first school district was formed in 1865, only four years after the establishment of Dakota Territory.

Today, a board of education supervises South Dakota's public schools. Appointed by the governor with senate approval, each member of the board serves an eight-year term. The state superintendent of schools serves as the board's administrative officer. Children must attend school from ages seven to sixteen or until they graduate from eighth grade.

Many post-secondary institutions serve South Dakota. State-run schools include the University of South Dakota, in Vermillion; South Dakota State University, in Brookings; South Dakota School of Mines and Technology, in Rapid City; Black Hills State University, in Spearfish; Dakota State University, in Madison; and Northern State University, in Aberdeen. Private schools include Augustana College, North American Baptist Seminary, and Sioux Falls College, all in Sioux Falls; Dakota Wesleyan University, in Mitchell; Huron College, in Huron; Mount Marty College, in Yankton; National College, in Rapid City; Presentation College, in Aberdeen; and Sinte Gleska College, in Rosebud.

ECONOMY AND INDUSTRY

Principal Products:
Agriculture: Wheat, sheep, beef cattle, hay, oats, barley, rye, hogs, flax, corn, sorghum, poultry, dairy products, sunflowers, soybeans
Manufacturing: Food processing, nonelectrical machinery, surgical instruments, electronic components, cooking appliances, newspapers, lumber and wood products, hot-air balloons, and stone, glass, leather, and clay products
Natural Resources: Gold, silver, uranium, clay, gravel, sand, feldspar, coal, granite, mica, beryl, limestone, bentonite, manganese, oil, gypsum, natural gas, lumber

Business: Agriculture dominates South Dakota's economy, as it has ever since territorial days. Most of the state's income comes from raising crops and livestock, or selling them to processors. More than two-thirds of the state's agricultural income comes from livestock. South Dakota ranks among the leading states in beef cattle and calves, hogs, sheep, and lambs. Dairy products and poultry are also important. Corn and wheat are the state's leading crops.

Meat-packing plants, dairies, and flour mills make food processing the top manufacturing industry. South Dakota also manufactures farm equipment, nonelectrical machinery, electronic components, and gold jewelry. Sioux Falls has the largest meat-processing plant in the state. Both Sioux Falls and Rapid City are major trade centers. The Coyote State boasts the largest gold mine in the Western Hemisphere, the Homestake Mine at Lead. The state produces about one-sixth of the nation's gold.

Communication: South Dakota has enjoyed an active press since territorial days. The region's first newspaper, the *Dakota Democrat*, was founded in Sioux Falls in 1859. Two years later, the *Yankton Press and Dakotan* started. It holds the honor of being the state's oldest continuous paper. Today, about 13 daily newspapers, 90 weeklies, and 13 periodicals are produced in South Dakota. Sioux Falls's *Argus-Leader* and the *Rapid City Journal* are the dailies with the largest circulations.

Transportation: Six different freight railroads use the state's 3,000 mi. (4,828 km) of track. South Dakota has more than 73,000 mi. (117,479 km) of roads, including about 765 mi. (1,231 km) of interstate highway. I-29 is a north-south route in the far-eastern part of the state. I-90 travels east-west and runs through the southern section of the state before turning northwest in the Black Hills.

South Dakota has about 79 public airports. The airports in Sioux Falls and Rapid City, which host several major airlines, serve the most passengers.

SOCIAL AND CULTURAL LIFE

Museums: South Dakotans preserve their heritage in museums throughout the state. Three of the largest museums are state supported. The W. H. Over Museum at the University of South Dakota in Vermillion contains extensive collections of Indian and pioneer artifacts, historical photographs, and mounted specimens of

A display at the Agricultural Heritage Museum in Brookings

animals and birds native to the Northern Great Plains. The Museum of Geology at the South Dakota School of Mines and Technology displays minerals, gems, and the fossilized bones of dinosaurs found in the state. The Agricultural Heritage Museum at South Dakota State University in Brookings portrays the historical development of South Dakota's agriculture.

The South Dakota Cultural Heritage Center in Pierre holds the collection of the South Dakota Historical Society, including the Vérendrye Plate. The Adams Memorial Museum in Deadwood exhibits artifacts from the gold-rush days. The Sioux Indian Museum and Crafts Center in Rapid City offers demonstrations of Native American crafts. The Pettigrew Home and Museum in Sioux Falls, the home of the state's first United States senator, has exhibits of the area's natural history and Native American history. The Friends of the Middle Border Museum of Pioneer Life in Mitchell contains tape recordings of folk songs, cowboy ballads, and Indian music, as well as a home, schoolhouse, and general store from the 1880s. The Old West Museum in Chamberlain displays an old-time Main Street, as well as antique guns, tractors, and glassware. Old Fort Meade Cavalry Museum in Sturgis is a restored fort that served the cavalry during the Sioux War of the 1870s. Dacotah Prairie Museum in Aberdeen portrays Indian and pioneer history. The Shrine to Music Museum, in Vermillion, houses more than three thousand musical instruments and related musical memorabilia.

Natural-history lovers may view five ecological zones at the Delbridge Museum of Natural History in Sioux Falls. The Call of the Wild Museum, in Hill City, displays hundreds of mounted American wildlife specimens. Art lovers can appreciate the state's two most famous artists at several locations. The Harvey Dunn Collection at the South Dakota Memorial Art Center in Brookings is the largest collection of this artist's works. The Oscar Howe Art Center, in Mitchell, and the Oscar Howe Gallery, in Vermillion, showcase many of Howe's paintings.

Libraries: In 1884, a handful of settlers united to create the Alexander Mitchell Library in Aberdeen, the state's first library. Today, South Dakota has about 150 public libraries and 14 bookmobiles. The largest by far is the University of South Dakota Library at Vermillion, with 500,000 volumes. South Dakota State University's library houses about 200,000 volumes. The State Library in Pierre serves as a valuable resource for South Dakota scholars.

Performing Arts: The Black Hills of South Dakota annually serve as the setting for the world-famous Black Hills Passion Play. For decades, South Dakotans and visitors have come to Spearfish to watch this dramatic interpretation of the last days of Christ. Spearfish actors also perform *Dakota Sal: Heroine of the Wild West,* at the Matthews Opera House.

The theme of the Wild West provides other opportunities for South Dakota drama. Deadwood hosts *The Trial of Jack McCall,* a street play about the trial of the man who killed Wild Bill Hickok. The Black Hills Playhouse in Custer State Park offers dramas, musicals, and comedies each summer.

South Dakotans enjoy Sioux Falls' Sioux Empire Youth Orchestra and the South Dakota Symphony, as well as Rapid City's Black Hills Symphony Orchestra. Country-and-western music can be heard at the Mountain Music Show in Custer, the Day County Fair in Webster, and the South Dakota and Open Fiddling Contest in Yankton. Traditional Sioux music is performed at powwows throughout the state.

Sports and Recreation: South Dakota has two professional basketball teams, the Skyforce in Sioux Falls, and the Rapid City Thrillers. Fans of college sports follow teams from the state's many schools, especially the University of South Dakota Coyotes and the South Dakota State Jackrabbits. Both schools are members of the North Central Intercollegiate Conference. South Dakota hosts many rodeos throughout the year.

Outdoors enthusiasts may enjoy hiking, climbing, and hunting in South Dakota. Natural and artificial lakes offer swimming, boating, fishing, and waterskiing. Downhill skiing in the Black Hills and near Sioux Falls, as well as cross-country trails in the state parks and the Black Hills National Forest, provide wintertime fun.

Historic Sites and Landmarks:

Dakota Territorial Museum, in Yankton, includes the restored Dakota Territorial Legislative Council Building and replicas of a general store, post office, dental office, blacksmith shop, and 1893 railway depot.

Hot Springs Historic District contains thirty-nine Romanesque-style buildings made of local sandstone.

Humphrey Drug Store, in Huron, owned by the family of former Vice-President Hubert H. Humphrey, maintains a 1930s atmosphere.

Mellette House, in Watertown, the home of South Dakota's first governor, includes the home's original furniture and family heirlooms.

Mount Moriah Cemetery, in Deadwood, is the final resting place of such colorful local characters as Wild Bill Hickok, Calamity Jane, Preacher Smith, and Seth Bullock.

Mount Rushmore National Memorial, near Keystone, is a massive stone carving of the likenesses of U.S. Presidents George Washington, Thomas Jefferson, Theodore Roosevelt, and Abraham Lincoln.

Prairie Village, near Madison, is a replica of an 1890s Great Plains pioneer town that includes restored buildings, antique vehicles, a steam train, and a summer theater.

Prehistoric Indian Village National Historic Landmark Archaeological Site, near Mitchell, allows visitors to view the remains of a thousand-year-old Indian village.

Rockerville Ghost Town, near Rapid City, is the replica of an 1878 mining camp.

Thunderhead Underground Falls, in Keystone, is the oldest gold-mining tunnel in the Black Hills that is open to the public.

Laura Ingalls Wilder Memorial, in De Smet, honors the author of the much-beloved "Little House" books.

Wounded Knee Battlefield, at Wounded Knee, commemorates the last major conflict between the Sioux and the U.S. Army.

Other Interesting Places to Visit:

Badlands National Park, in western South Dakota, contains multicolored peaks, spirals, and gullies formed over millions of years by wind and water erosion.

Badlands Petrified Gardens, in Kadoka, displays Badlands minerals, prehistoric fossils, dinosaur tracks, and petrified tree trunks.

D. C. Booth Historic Fish Hatchery, in Spearfish, is the oldest fish hatchery in the West. Trout raised at the hatchery are used to stock Black Hills streams.

Chapel in the Hills, near Rapid City, is a replica of an 800-year-old Norwegian wooden church.

Corn Palace, in Mitchell, displays elaborate murals created annually from multicolored corn and other grains.

Crazy Horse Memorial, near Custer, a massive sculptural rendering of the famous Oglala chief, is being carved out of a granite mountain. When completed, it will be the largest sculpture in the world.

The Laura Ingalls Wilder Memorial in De Smet

Dinosaur Park, in Rapid City, contains seven life-size sculptures of prehistoric reptiles that roamed what is now South Dakota.

EROS (Earth Resources Observation System), near Garretson, is a processing point for millions of photographs of the earth taken from aircraft and satellites.

Evans Plunge, in Hot Springs, is the largest natural warm-water indoor pool in the world.

Geographical Center of the United States is located near Castle Rock in the western part of the state.

Harney Peak, in Pennington County in the Black Hills, is the highest point in the United States east of the Rocky Mountains.

Homestake Mine, in Lead, is the largest gold-producing mine in the Western Hemisphere. Tours of surface mining activities are available.

State Capitol, in Pierre, is built of Bedford limestone, local boulder, and granite, and was completed in 1910.

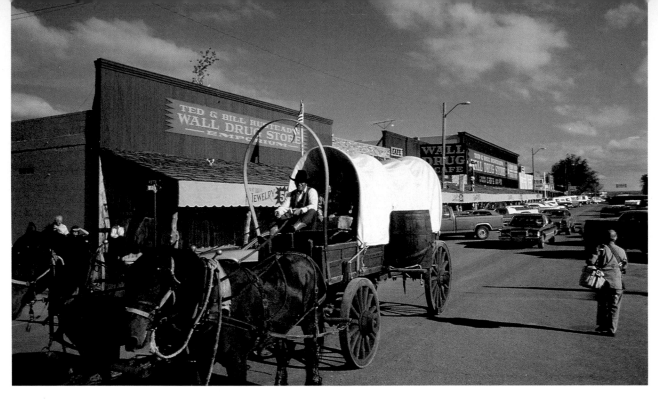

The world-famous Wall Drug Store in Wall

Trail of the Spirits, near Sisseton, is a registered National Recreation Trail in Sica Hollow State Park.

Wall Drug Store, in Wall, is a world-famous pharmacy, entertainment center, souvenir store, and restaurant.

IMPORTANT DATES

c. 8000-5000 B.C.—Nomadic groups live in South Dakota

c. A.D. 500-800—Seminomadic Mound Builders thrive in present-day South Dakota

c. 1500—The Arikara, the first Native Americans to be described in written records, move into South Dakota

1682—René-Robert Cavelier, Sieur de La Salle, claims all land drained by the Mississippi River system, including the land of present-day South Dakota, for France

1700s—The Sioux, or Dakota, begin moving into present-day South Dakota

1743—François and Louis Joseph La Vérendrye, looking for a water route to the Pacific Ocean, bury an inscribed lead plate near present-day Fort Pierre

1762—France cedes its land west of the Mississippi River to Spain

1775—Pierre Dorion, a French-Canadian fur trader, marries a Yankton Sioux woman and becomes the first permanent white settler in present-day South Dakota

1794—Jean Baptiste Trudeau builds winter quarters—the first house in the Dakotas—on the Missouri River near the subsequent site of Fort Randall

1800—Spain returns western lands drained by the Mississippi to France

1803—The U.S. buys present-day South Dakota from France as part of the Louisiana Purchase

1804-06—The Lewis and Clark expedition passes through South Dakota on its way toward the Pacific Ocean

1809—Manuel Lisa organizes local fur trade between the St. Louis Fur Company and Indians along the Missouri River

1812—The land of present-day South Dakota becomes part of Missouri Territory; the Sioux join the British against the Americans in the War of 1812

1815—The Sioux sign a peace treaty with the U.S.

1817—Joseph La Framboise establishes South Dakota's first permanent white settlement at what is now Fort Pierre

1823—The first large-scale military action against South Dakota's Indians begins when troops led by General William Ashley are attacked by the Arikara

1825—General Henry Atkinson and Colonel Benjamin O'Fallon negotiate peace treaties with Teton Sioux tribes

1831—The *Yellowstone*, the first steamboat on the Missouri River, paddles to Fort Tecumseh (present-day Fort Pierre)

1851—The Santee Sioux cede all lands east of the Big Sioux River to the U.S.

1857—Iowa businessmen plan the present-day city of Sioux Falls

1858—The Yankton Sioux sell 14 million acres (6 million hectares) of land between the Big Sioux and Missouri rivers for 12 cents per acre

1861—Dakota Territory is established; it includes present-day North and South Dakota, as well as much of present-day Wyoming and Montana; Yankton becomes the territorial capital

1862—The U.S. government forces Santee Sioux from Minnesota into Dakota Territory after a Sioux uprising fails; Territorial Governor William Jayne signs a bill to set up the first public schools in the territory

1864—The creation of Montana Territory removes the northwestern portion of Dakota Territory

1866—Sioux Indians attack federal troops sent to survey a road through the Powder River country to the goldfields in Montana, resulting in Chief Red Cloud's War

1868—The Fort Laramie Treaty ends Chief Red Cloud's War by creating the Great Sioux Reservation west of the Missouri River; the formation of Wyoming Territory limits the boundaries of Dakota Territory to present-day North and South Dakota

1873—The Dakota Southern Railroad, the first railroad in the territory, reaches Yankton

1874—American troops led by General George Armstrong Custer discover gold in the Black Hills

1876—The Sioux War breaks out as the Sioux attempt to keep prospectors out of the Black Hills; the Sioux cede the Black Hills region to the federal government; lawman and gunfighter James Butler "Wild Bill" Hickok is shot to death during a poker game in Deadwood

1877—George Hearst buys the Homestake Mine for $70,000; Fort Meade opens

1878—Pioneering farmers begin the rush for land known as the "Great Dakota Boom"

1879—Movement for Dakota statehood begins

1881—The melting of snow after an extremely severe winter causes floods that ravage South Dakota; the Congregational church founds the first institution of higher learning (Yankton College) in present-day South Dakota

1882—The University of South Dakota opens at Vermillion

1888—A paralyzing blizzard causes hundreds of deaths; Republicans make the issue of the admission of Dakota Territory as two separate states part of their election campaign; South Dakotans vote to make Pierre the state capital

1889—The U.S. Congress splits Dakota Territory in half and North Dakota and South Dakota enter the Union as the thirty-ninth and fortieth states; the remaining Sioux land west of the Missouri is split into four smaller reservations; an eclipse of the sun causes Wovoka, a Paiute Indian leader in Nevada, to go into a trance, from which he receives the idea of the Ghost Dance

1890—The Ghost Dance movement spreads to South Dakota and alarms whites; at Wounded Knee, government troops massacre more than 200 surrendering Sioux men, women and children, ending the Ghost Dance movement

1898—South Dakota becomes the first state to pass an initiative and referendum law

1900—A fire destroys $250,000 worth of property in Lead

1903—Mitchell erects a capitol building, hoping to wrest the state capital from Pierre

1909—John Morrell and Company opens a meat-packing plant in Sioux Falls

1910—The present-day capitol building in Pierre is completed

1917—Progressive Governor Peter Norbeck begins policies to end railroad monopolies and to lower passenger rates; legislation is passed permitting the state to extend loans to farmers

1918—Sixteen of seventeen Hutterite colonies, whose members refuse to support World War I, flee to Canada

1922—Hamlin Garland wins the Pulitzer Prize in biography for *A Daughter of the Middle Border*

1927—Work begins on Mount Rushmore National Memorial; President Calvin Coolidge spends the summer in the Black Hills

1930—The worst grasshopper plague in South Dakota's history begins

1932—The Democrats win every state office for the first time; farm foreclosures reach their peak at 3,864; farm organizations exert pressure to prevent further foreclosures

1934—The Indian Reorganization Act restores cultural activities among the Sioux

1935—*Explorer II*, a balloon, is launched from Stratosphere Bowl near Rapid City, and soars a record-breaking 13 mi. (21 km) into the stratosphere

1938—Workers finish the first oil-topped highway across South Dakota

1939—South Dakota native Ernest Lawrence wins the Nobel Prize in physics for the invention of the cyclotron; President Franklin D. Roosevelt creates Badlands National Park

1941—Work on Mount Rushmore National Memorial is halted

1944—The Flood Control Act provides for dams along the Missouri River

1947—Governor George T. Mickelson begins the largest construction and public-works program in the state's history

1948—Korczak Ziolkowski begins work on the Crazy Horse Memorial

1954—The state's first commercial oil well is drilled in Harding County

1956—Fort Randall Dam, the first of South Dakota's Missouri River dams, is completed; Democrat George McGovern is elected to Congress

1963—The federal government installs 150 Minuteman missiles near Wall; the Fischer quintuplets are born in Aberdeen

1964—Oahe Dam, the largest Missouri River dam in South Dakota, is completed; South Dakota native Hubert H. Humphrey becomes vice-president under Lyndon Johnson

1966—The Pathfinder Atomic Power Plant near Sioux Falls begins producing electricity

1968—Humphrey loses to Richard Nixon in a close presidential election

1970—The United Sioux Tribes Development Corporation is chartered to assist members in relocating and finding jobs outside of the reservations

1972—South Dakota Senator George McGovern loses a landslide presidential election to Richard Nixon; Rapid City's Canyon Lake Dam bursts, killing 238 people and causing $100 million in damage

1973—About 200 armed members of the American Indian Movement (AIM) occupy Wounded Knee to protest policies towards Native Americans

1980—The U.S. Supreme Court upholds compensation of $22.5 million for land in the Black Hills taken from the Sioux by the federal government in 1877

1989—South Dakota celebrates its centennial with programs, parades, and two wagon trains that travel throughout the state and meet in Huron at the South Dakota State Fair

1990—Ceremonies are held to observe the one-hundredth anniversary of the massacre at Wounded Knee

1991—Several of South Dakota's Indian reservations receive federal funds to help reduce the high infant mortality rate

1993—Governor George S. Mickelson is killed in a plane crash in eastern Iowa

IMPORTANT PEOPLE

James Abdnor (1923-   ), born in Kennebec; politician; U.S. representative from South Dakota (1973-81); U.S. senator (1981-87); chaired the Senate Water Resources Subcommittee; represented the state in disputes about the use of water from the Missouri River

James Abourezk (1931-   ), born in Wood; politician; U.S. representative from South Dakota (1971-73); first Arab American elected to the U.S. Senate (1973-79); championed Indian rights; frequently led opposition to the Nixon administration

JAMES ABOUREZK

Edith Ammons (1884-1959), and **Ida Mary Ammons** (18?-19?), pioneers; in 1907, homesteaded 30 mi. (48 km) southeast of Pierre; built the Ammons empire, which included the town of Ammons and the newspaper *Reservation Wand*

George Lee (Sparky) Anderson (1934-   ), born in Bridgewater; professional baseball player and manager; became the first manager to win the World Series in both the National and American leagues; led the Cincinnati Reds to two World Series, four pennants, and five division titles in nine years; led the Detroit Tigers to two division titles and the 1984 World Series

SPARKY ANDERSON

Floyd Franklin Bannister (1955-   ), born in Pierre; professional baseball player; pitcher who led the American League in strikeouts with the 1982 Seattle Mariners; posted a 13-1 second-half record while leading the Chicago White Sox to the American League West title in 1983

Lyman Frank (L. Frank) Baum (1856-1919), author, newspaper editor; edited Aberdeen's *Saturday Pioneer;* wrote *The Wonderful Wizard of Oz* and many other stories set in the mythical land of Oz

L. FRANK BAUM

William Henry Harrison Beadle (1838-1915), soldier, educator; surveyor general of Dakota Territory (1869); as superintendent of public instruction (1879-85), greatly increased the number of schools in the territory; worked to protect inexpensive lands the government had set aside for schools

Gutzon Borglum (1867-1941), sculptor; created a world-famous monument by carving likenesses of Presidents Washington, Jefferson, Theodore Roosevelt, and Lincoln on Mount Rushmore; sculpted the bust of Lincoln in the rotunda of the U.S. Capitol

Lincoln Borglum (1912-1986), sculptor, photographer; worked with his father and later supervised the Mount Rushmore project; published many photographs

GUTZON BORGLUM

TOM BROKAW

CALAMITY JANE

DAVE COLLINS

GEORGE CUSTER

Tom Brokaw (1940-   ), born in Webster; broadcast journalist; NBC's White House correspondent (1973-76); host of the "Today" show (1976-82); became anchor of the "NBC Nightly News" in 1982

Seth Bullock (1840?-1919), law officer; organized Theodore Roosevelt's Rough Riders; served under Roosevelt as U.S. marshall for South Dakota; rode the range as a cowboy for big ranch outfits; frightened Deadwood's outlaws as the sheriff of Lawrence County

Charles Henry Burke (1862-1944), politician, public official; U.S. representative from South Dakota (1899-1907, 1909-15); improved education and health care for Native Americans as commissioner of Indian affairs (1921-29)

Martha Jane (Calamity Jane) Burke (1851-1903), army scout; became a legendary Wild West heroine; starred in Buffalo Bill's Wild West Show; buried in Mount Moriah Cemetery

Francis Higbee Case (1896-1962), politician, journalist; edited and published several South Dakota newspapers; U.S. representative from South Dakota (1937-51); U.S. senator (1951-62); sponsored legislation that created the interstate highway system

Pierre Chouteau, Jr. (1789-1865), fur trader; became one of the most powerful financiers of his day; pioneered the use of steamboats on the Missouri River in the fur trade; South Dakota's state capital is named for him

Charles Badger Clark (1883-1957), lived in Custer; served as poet laureate of South Dakota for many years; wrote such collections of poems as *Sun and Saddle Leather, Sky Lines and Wood Smoke,* and *Spike*; most famous poems include "The Job," "The Glory Trail," and "A Cowboy's Prayer"

Amanda Clement (1888-1971), born in Hudson; baseball umpire; was baseball's first woman umpire; is recognized at the Baseball Hall of Fame at Cooperstown, New York, the Women's Sports Hall of Fame, and the Women's Sports Foundation in San Francisco; inducted into South Dakota Hall of Fame (1982)

David Scott Collins (1952-   ), born in Rapid City; professional baseball player; speedy outfielder who starred with many teams; hit over .300 three times; stole 79 bases with the 1980 Cincinnati Reds and 60 bases with the 1984 Toronto Blue Jays

Crazy Horse (1849?-1877), Oglala chief; led the Teton Sioux in the defense of the Black Hills; fought in the Battle of the Little Big Horn; defeated General George Crook at the Battle of the Rosebud; died resisting arrest

George Armstrong Custer (1839-1876), soldier; led the military expedition that discovered gold in the Black Hills; died in the Battle of the Little Big Horn in Montana

Thomas A. Daschle (1947-   ), born in Aberdeen, politician; U.S. representative from South Dakota (1979-87); U.S. senator (1987-   ); co-chair of the Senate Democratic Policy Committee; promoted compensation for Vietnam Agent Orange victims

THOMAS DASCHLE

Harvey Dunn (1884-1952), born near De Smet; artist; portrayed prairie life in South Dakota and American troops during World War I; for many years, did illustrations for the *Saturday Evening Post* and *American Legion* magazine

Myron Floren (1919-   ), born in Webster; musician; played the accordion for years on "The Lawrence Welk Show"

Mary Hallock Foote (1847-1938), author, illustrator; lived in Deadwood in the 1880s; wrote and illustrated many tales of western life; wrote *The Led-Horse Claim*

Terry Jay Forster (1952-   ), born in Sioux Falls; professional baseball player; burned the fastball past enemy batters as a relief pitcher with the Chicago White Sox, Los Angeles Dodgers, and other teams; led the American League with 24 saves in 1974

JOSEPH FOSS

Joseph J. Foss (1915-   ), born in Sioux Falls; aviator, politician; won the Congressional Medal of Honor for shooting down 31 enemy aircraft in World War II; received Distinguished Flying Cross from Admiral Halsey; governor of South Dakota (1955-59)

John Charles Frémont (1813-1890), explorer; traveled throughout the western United States, earning the nickname the "Pathfinder"; visited the Dakota region in 1838 and named several lakes in present-day South Dakota, including Lakes Poinsett and Benton

Gall (1840?-1894), born near the Moreau River; Hunkpapa war chief; played an important role in the defeat of Custer at the Battle of the Little Big Horn; settled on the Standing Rock Reservation and helped influence his people to accept the government's plans to educate Indian children

GALL

Hamlin Garland (1860-1940), author; wrote books dealing with rural life on the prairie near Aberdeen, including *Main Travelled Roads* and *A Son of the Middle Border*; won the 1922 Pulitzer Prize in biography for *A Daughter of the Middle Border*

Robert W. Haire (1845-1916), Catholic priest, reformer; moved to Dakota Territory in 1880; founded a hospital at Aberdeen, edited a labor newspaper and encouraged the farm movement; active in the successful movement for an initiative and referendum law

Niels Ebbeson Hansen (1866-1960), agriculturalist; searched the world for grains that would grow in South Dakota's semi-arid environment; introduced Cossack wheat, crested wheat grass, and Anoka apple to the state; taught at State College of Agriculture and Mechanical Arts and directed State Agriculture Experimental Station

HAMLIN GARLAND

RICHARD HARKNESS

OSCAR HOWE

HUBERT H. HUMPHREY

WILLIAM JANKLOW

William Hobart Hare (1838-1909), missionary; established schools and missions while serving as the Protestant Episcopal missionary bishop to the Sioux (1872-83); Bishop of Dakota (1883-1909)

Richard Harkness (1907-   ), born in Artesian; journalist; hosted "Story of the Week," one of the first network news interview programs

Mary Hart (1950-   ), born in Sioux Falls; network television personality; host of the syndicated television program "Entertainment Tonight"

James Butler (Wild Bill) Hickok (1837-1876), hunter, trapper, soldier, scout, and law officer; served as the marshall of several rough Kansas towns (1869-72); toured with Buffalo Bill's Wild West Show (1872-73); moved to "clean up" Deadwood in 1876 but was shot to death by Jack McCall; buried in Mount Moriah Cemetery

Oscar Howe (1915-1983), born on the Crow Creek Reservation; artist; painted and drew works influenced by and depicting his Sioux heritage; displayed his works in New York, San Francisco, London, and Paris; taught as artist-in-residence at the University of South Dakota (1957-83); painted murals in many locations, including the Oscar Howe Art Center in Mitchell and Mobridge's Municipal Auditorium; designed the exterior panels of the Corn Palace (1948-71)

Hubert Horatio Humphrey (1911-1978), born in Wallace; politician, statesman; worked as a pharmacist in his father's Huron drugstore during the depression before finishing his degree at the University of Minnesota; U.S. senator from Minnesota (1949-65, 1971-78); vice-president under Lyndon Johnson (1965-69); made three unsuccessful bids for the Democratic presidential nomination; won the nomination in 1968, but lost the election to Richard Nixon; championed many social and civil-rights reforms

William J. Janklow (1939-   ), politician; became the first South Dakotan to serve two four-year terms as governor (1979-87); gained a reputation as an opponent of Indian claims

Timothy Johnson (1946-   ), born in Canton; politician; U.S. representative from South Dakota (1986-   ); is credited with passing eight different pieces of legislation in his first term, including three South Dakota water projects; won a near-record 72 percent of the vote in 1988

Herbert Krause (1905-1976), author, educator; lived in Sioux Falls and taught at Augustana College; wrote novels about western life, including *The Thresher* and *Wind Without Rain*

Cheryl Ladd (1951-   ), born Cheryl Stoppelmoor in Huron; actress; performed first as a voice in cartoons, later acted in commercials; starred in the television series "Charlie's Angels"

Rose Wilder Lane (1887-1968), born in De Smet; author; daughter of Laura Ingalls Wilder; wrote the "Ernestine" series of stories for the *Saturday Evening Post*; her novels *Let the Hurricane Roar* and *Old Home Town* portrayed life in South Dakota

Ernest O. Lawrence (1901-1958), born in Canton; physicist; invented the cyclotron, the world's first atom-smasher; won the Nobel Prize in physics (1939); played a major role in the development of the atomic bomb

ERNEST LAWRENCE

Manuel Lisa (1772-1820), fur trader, merchant; organized the Missouri Fur Company (1808); traded extensively in the Dakota region; became the U.S. government agent to the Indians on the upper Missouri River (1814) and secured their help against the British in the War of 1812

Frederick Manfred (1912-   ), author; portrayed the Sioux in *Conquering Horse* and *Scarlet Plume*; depicted the Black Hills gold rush in *King of Spades*; writer-in-residence at the University of South Dakota (1968-   )

George S. McGovern (1922-   ), born in Avon; politician, educator; taught history and political science at Dakota Wesleyan University (1949-53); U.S. representative from South Dakota (1957-61); U.S. senator (1963-81); became a leading critic of the war in Vietnam; won the Democratic nomination for the presidency in 1972, but lost to Richard Nixon in a landslide election

GEORGE McGOVERN

Arthur C. Mellette (1842-1896), politician; last territorial governor of Dakota Territory (1885-89) and first state governor of South Dakota (1889-93)

George T. Mickelson (1903-1965), born in Selby; politician; governor of South Dakota (1949-51); promoted highway construction and the development of the Missouri River; later served as a federal judge

William Mervin (Billy) Mills (1938-   ), born in Pine Ridge; track-and-field athlete; during the 1964 Olympics, became the first American ever to win the 10,000-meter race; later reactivated the American Indian Athletic Hall of Fame; founded the Billy Mills Leadership Institute; his career was depicted in the film *Running Brave*

GEORGE MICKELSON

Karl Earl Mundt (1900-1974), born in Humboldt; politician; U.S. representative from South Dakota (1938-48); U.S. senator (1949-72); led anti-Communist attacks as chairman of the House Un-American Activities Committee

Allen Neuharth (1924-   ), born in Eureka; businessman; founded the newspaper *USA Today* in 1982; former chairman of Gannett Company Inc.

BILLY MILLS

LARRY PRESSLER

GLADYS PYLE

RED CLOUD

BEN REIFEL

Peter Norbeck (1870-1936), born near Vermillion; politician; governor of South Dakota (1917-21); as governor, began policies to end monopolies, lower railroad prices, and maintain farm prices; as a U.S. senator (1921-36), promoted the development of Custer State Park, Mount Rushmore National Memorial, and Badlands National Monument

Pat O'Brien (1948-   ), born in Sioux Falls; network television sports personality

Gary Owens (1936-   ), born in Mitchell; actor; portrayed the announcer on the television program ''Laugh-In''; served as a voice for many cartoon shows and narrated several comedy albums

Richard Franklin Pettigrew (1848-1926), politician; led the development of Sioux Falls; territorial delegate to the U.S. House of Representatives (1881-83); one of the first two U.S. senators from South Dakota (1889-1901); worked to preserve the state's publicly owned forests

Scotty Philip (1858-1911), helped preserve America's buffalo; immigrated to South Dakota from Scotland at age 16; rounded up the 57 surviving buffalo along the Cheyenne River and sheltered them in a fenced pasture along the Missouri River near Pierre; the herd grew to 1,000 by the time of his death and became the source of all modern-day herds

Larry Pressler (1942-   ), born in Sioux Falls; politician; U.S. representative from South Dakota (1975-79); U.S. senator (1979-   ); sponsored bills on many issues relating to the state

Gladys Pyle (1890-1989), politician, teacher, businesswoman; first female member of the South Dakota House of Representatives (1923-27); first woman elected to U.S. Senate from South Dakota (elected to fill the remaining two months of Peter Norbeck's term), (1938-39); South Dakota secretary of state (1927-31); gubernatorial candidate (1930)

Red Cloud (1822-1909), Oglala chief; through the Laramie Treaty (1868) following Chief Red Cloud's War, forced U.S. Army troops to abandon forts and roads that might have endangered buffalo herds

Ben Reifel (1906-1990), born near Parmalee; politician; U.S. representative from South Dakota (1961-71); a Brûlé Sioux, he was the only Native American member of Congress in the post-World War II era; president of American Indian National Bank; executive officer for the Bureau of Indian Affairs

Joe Robbie (1916-1990), born in Sisseton; lawyer, businessman; owner of the National Football League's Miami Dolphins; built Joe Robbie Stadium in Miami; received 1979 Horatio Alger Award

Doane Robinson (1856-1946), historian; first major historian of South Dakota and the Sioux; served as state historian for a quarter century; conceived the idea for Mount Rushmore National Memorial

Ole Edvart Rölvaag (1876-1931), author, educator; novelist; lived in Canton; described the plight of Norwegian-American farmers in Dakota Territory in his novel *Giants in the Earth;* also wrote *Peder Victorious* and *Their Father's God;* taught Norwegian at St. Olaf College in Minnesota

OLE RÖLVAAG

Earl Sande (1898-1968), born in Groton; jockey; won the colorful nicknames "The Dutchman" and "Handy Guy"; won 968 races riding such famous horses as Man o' War and Gallant Fox; won horseracing's Triple Crown on Gallant Fox in 1930; named to the Jockey's Hall of Fame; considered by some to have been the greatest jockey in history

Theodore W. Schultz (1902-   ), born in Arlington; economist; author of many books on economics; professor at the University of Chicago; won the 1979 Nobel Prize in Economics

EARL SANDE

Sitting Bull (1834?-1890), born near Grand River; Hunkpapa Sioux medicine man and spiritual leader; during the Sioux War of 1876, was one of the leaders of Sioux forces that crushed General Custer's forces at the Battle of the Little Bighorn in Montana; in 1883, settled on the Standing Rock Reservation; traveled with Buffalo Bill's Wild West Show (1885); in 1890, when the U.S. government was trying to stop the Ghost Dance movement, was killed while being arrested by reservation police

Preacher Smith (1836?-1876), born Henry Weston Smith; Methodist minister; preached on street corners in Deadwood and rode the countryside as an itinerant preacher; died in the Black Hills, supposedly killed by Indians; buried in Mount Moriah Cemetery

SITTING BULL

Anne D. Tallent (1827-1901), settler, author; journeyed to the Black Hills in 1875, where she was the first white woman; wrote *Black Hills: The Last Hunting Ground of the Dakotas* (1900)

Casey Tibbs (1929-1990), born in Mission Ridge, world champion saddle bronc rider; Professional Rodeo Cowboys Association's all-around champion (1951); won six Saddle Bronc Riding crowns; was featured on the cover of *Life* magazine in 1951; stuntman in movies and on television

Norman Van Brocklin (1926-1983), born in Eagle Butte; professional football player and coach; quarterbacked the Los Angeles Rams to its only NFL championship (1951); retired after leading the Philadelphia Eagles to an NFL title in 1960; later coached the Minnesota Vikings and the Atlanta Falcons; elected to the National Football Hall of Fame

ANNE TALLENT

MAMIE VAN DOREN

STEWART WHITE

Mamie Van Doren (1933-   ), born Joan Lucille Olander in Rowena; actress; starred in 1950s and 1960s films such as *Ain't Misbehavin'*, *High School Confidential*, *College Confidential*, and *The Candidate*

Joseph Ward (1838-1889), minister, civil leader; began missionary work in Yankton (1869); participated in the 1883 and 1885 state constitutional conventions; designed the state seal; founded and served as first president of Yankton College (1882-89)

Stewart Edward White (1873-1946), author; used the mining community of Keystone as the setting for such novels as *The Westerners* and *The Claim Jumpers*; left Keystone in the early 1900s after local residents took offense at the descriptions of themselves in his novels

Laura Ingalls Wilder (1867-1957), author; wrote *Little House on the Prairie* and seven other "Little House" books based on her life on the frontier; several of the books, including *The Long Winter* and *Little House on the Prairie*, describe her years in De Smet

Korczak Ziolkowski (1909-1982), sculptor; worked briefly with the Borglums on the Mount Rushmore National Memorial; spent more than 30 years carving a gigantic sculpture of Chief Crazy Horse out of Thunderhead Mountain; sculpted the Sitting Bull monument in Mobridge and the Wild Bill Hickok monument in Deadwood

GOVERNORS

Arthur C. Mellette	1889-1893	Sigurd Anderson	1951-1955
Charles H. Sheldon	1893-1897	Joseph J. Foss	1955-1959
Andrew E. Lee	1897-1901	Ralph Herseth	1959-1961
Charles N. Herreid	1901-1905	Archie Gubbrud	1961-1965
Samuel H. Elrod	1905-1907	Nils A. Boe	1965-1969
Coe I. Crawford	1907-1909	Frank L. Farrar	1969-1971
Robert S. Vessey	1909-1913	Richard F. Kneip	1971-1978
Frank M. Byrne	1913-1917	Harvey L. Wollman	1978-1979
Peter Norbeck	1917-1921	William J. Janklow	1979-1987
William H. McMaster	1921-1925	George S. Mickelson	1987-1993
Carl Gunderson	1925-1927	Walter Dale Miller	1993-1994
William J. Bulow	1927-1931	William J. Janklow	1994-
Warren E. Green	1931-1933		
Thomas Berry	1933-1937		
Leslie Jensen	1937-1939		
Harlan J. Bushfield	1939-1943		
Merrell Q. Sharpe	1943-1947		
George T. Mickelson	1947-1951		

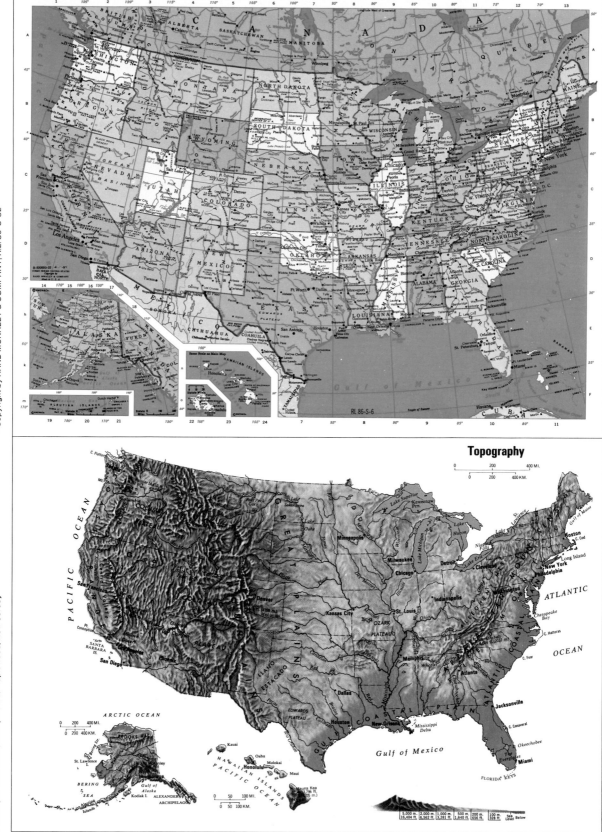

Topography

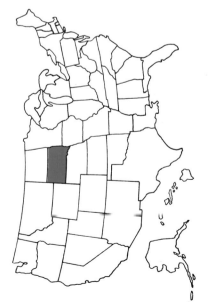

MAP KEY

Aberdeen B7
Alcester D9
Alexandria D8
Allen D4
Alpena C7
Altamont C9
Amherst B8
Andes Lake D7
Andover B8
Angostura Reservoir D2
Arlington C8
Armor C8
Artesian C7
Ashton C7
Astoria C9
Athol C7
Aurora C9
Avon E7
Bad River C5
Badger C8
Badlands National Park D3
Baltic D9
Barnard B7
Batesland D3
Bath B8
Belle Fourche C2
Belle Fourche Reservoir C2
Belle Fourche River C2
Belvidere D4
Beresford D9
Big Stone Lake B9
Big Sioux River E9
Big Stone City B9
Bison B3
Bitter Lake B8
Black Hawk C2
Black Hills National Forest C2
Blunt C6
Bon Homme Colony E8
Bonesteel D7
Bonilla C7
Bowdle B6
Box Elder C2
Bradley B8
Brandon D9
Brandt C9
Brentford B7
Bridgewater D8
Bristol B8
Britton B7
Broadland C7
Brookings C9
Bruce C9
Bryant C8
Buffalo A2
Buffalo Gap D2
Buffalo B2
Bull Creek B4
Burbank E9
Burke D6
Bushnell C9
Camp Crook B2

Canistota D8
Canova D9
Canton D9
Carthage C8
Castlewood C9
Cavour C7
Centerville D8
Central City C2
Chamberlain D7
Chancellor D8
Cherry Creek C4
Chester C9
Cheyenne River Indian Reservation C4
Cheyenne River C4
Claire City B8
Claremont B8
Clark C8
Clay Creek E7
Clear Lake C9
Colman C8
Colome D6
Colton D9
Columbia B7
Conde C7
Corona B8
Corsica D7
Corson D9
Cresbard C7
Crocker B8
Crooks D9
Crow Creek Indian Reservation D6
Custer State Park D2
Custer D2
Custer National Forest B3
Dallas D6
Dante D7
Davis D8
De Smet C8
Deadwood C2
Delmont D7
Dempster C8
Dimock D7
Doland C7
Draper D5
Dupree C4
East Sioux Falls D9
Eden B8
Edgemont D2
Egan C9
Elk Point E9
Elk Creek C2
Elkton C9
Ellis D9
Elm Springs Colony C3
Emery D8
Epiphany D8
Erwin C8
Estelline C9
Ethan D8
Eureka B6
Fairfax D6
Fairview B2

Faith B3
Faulkton B6
Fedora C8
Ferney B7
Flandreau Indian Reservation C9
Flandreau C9
Florence B8
Forestburg C8
Fort Pierre C5
Fort Thompson C6
Francis Case, Lake D6
Frankfort C7
Frederick B7
Freeman D8
Froehlich Addition D9
Fruitdale C2
Fulton D8
Ganvalley C7
Garden City B8
Garretson D9
Gary C9
Gayville E8
Geddes D7
Gettysburg B6
Glendale Colony C8
Glenham C8
Goodwin B6
Grand River B4
Greenwood D6
Gregory E7
Grenville B8
Groton D9
Harney Peak C2
Harrisburg D9
Harrison D2
Harrold C6

Lower Brule C6
Lower Brule Indian Reservation C5
Lyons D9
Madison D8
Manderson D3
Mansfield B7
Maple River A7
Marion D8
Martin D4
Marty E7
Marvin B8
Maxwell Colony D9
McCook Lake E9
McIntosh B4
McLaughlin B4
Meckling E8
Mellette B7
Menno D8
Midland C4
Milbank B9
Miller Dale Colony C8
Miller C6
Mission C7
Mission Hill D7
Missouri River C5
Mitchell D5
Mobridge B5
Monroe D8
Montrose D8
Moreau River B3
Morningside C7
Morristown B4
Mound City B6
Mount Vernon D7
Mount Rushmore National Memorial D2
Murdo D5
New Holland D7
New Underwood C3
New Effington B9
Newell C2
Nisland C2
Norris C8
North Sioux City D8
North Eagle Butte B5
Northville B7
Nunda C8
Oacoma D6
Oahe, Lake C6
Oelrichs D2
Oglala D4
Okreek D6
Oldham C8
Olivet D7
Onaka B6
Onida C6
Oral D2
Orient C7
Ortley B8
Pactola Reservoir C2
Parker D8
Parkston D7
Parmelee D5
Peever B8
Philip C4
Pickstown D7
Piedmont C2
Pierpont B7
Pierre C6
Pine Ridge D4
Pine Ridge Indian Reservation D4
Plankinton D7
Platte D7
Pollock B5
Poinsett, Lake C8
Ponca Creek D6
Porcupine D3
Potato Creek C3
Prairie City B3
Presho D5
Pringle D2
Provo D2
Pukwana D6
Quinn C4
Ramona C8
Rapid City C2
Ravinia D7
Raymond B8
Red Scaffold C3
Redfield C7
Ree Heights C6
Reliance D6
Renner D8
Revillo B9
Rockham C7
Roscoe B6
Rosebud D5
Rosebud Indian Reservation D5

Rosholt B9
Roslyn B8
Rowena D9
Rutland C9
Salem D8
Scotland D8
Selby B6
Seneca B3
Shadehill Reservoir C9
Sharpe, Lake C9
Sherman D8
Sinai C8
Sioux Falls D9
Sisseton B8
Sisseton Indian Reservation B9
Sisseton C2
South Shore C7
Spearfish E8
Spencer D6
Spink Colony D5
Springfield C7
St. Charles C2
St. Lawrence B4
St. Onge D7
Standing Rock Indian Reservation B9
Stickney D7
Stockholm C7
Storla B8
Strandburg B9
Stratford B7
Sturgis C2
Summit B8
Sunnyview C9
Tabor E8
Tea D9
Terraville C2
Timber Lake B3
Tolstoy B6
Toronto C9
Trail City B5
Traverse, Lake B9
Trent C9
Tripp D8
Tschetter Colony D8
Tulare B7
Turton B8
Twin Brooks C9
Tyndall E8
Utica E8
Vale D7
Valley Springs D9
Veblen B8
Vermillion E9
Vermillion River D8
Viborg D8
Vienna C8
Vivian D5
Volga C8
Volin E8
Wagner D7
Wakonda D8
Wakpala B5
Wall C3
Wallace C8
Wanblee D4
Warner B7
Wasta C3
Watauga B4
Watertown C8
Waubay B8
Waubay Lake B8
Webster B8
Wecota B6
Wentworth C8
Wessington C7
Wessington Springs C7
Westport B7
White River D5
White Lake D7
White C9
Whitehorse B5
Whitewood C2
Willow Lake C8
Wilmot B9
Wind Cave National Park D2
Winfred C8
Winner D6
Wolsey C7
Wood D5
Woonsocket C7
Worthing D9
Wounded Knee D3
Witten D5
Yale C8
Yankton Indian Reservation E8
Yankton E8
Zell C7

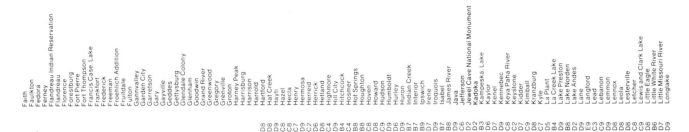

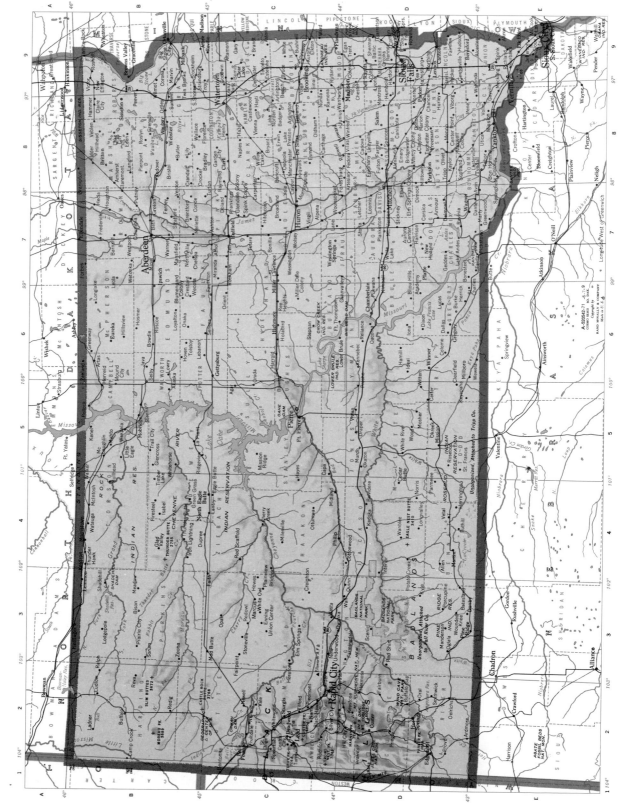

From *Cosmopolitan World Atlas* © 1990 by Rand McNally, R.L. 90-S-252

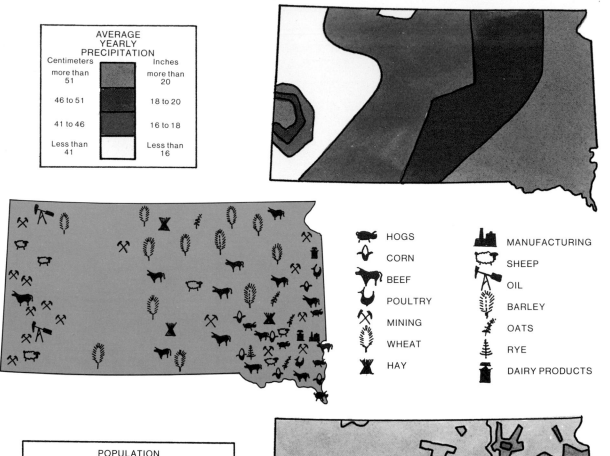

AVERAGE YEARLY PRECIPITATION

Centimeters		Inches
more than 51		more than 20
46 to 51		18 to 20
41 to 46		16 to 18
Less than 41		Less than 16

HOGS

CORN

BEEF

POULTRY

MINING

WHEAT

HAY

MANUFACTURING

SHEEP

OIL

BARLEY

OATS

RYE

DAIRY PRODUCTS

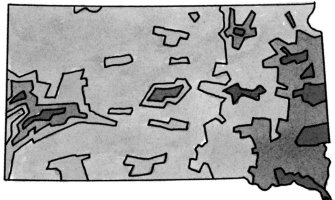

POPULATION DENSITY

Number of persons per square kilometer		Number of persons per square mile
more than 10		more than 25
4 to 10		10 to 25
2 to 4		5 to 10
Less than 2		Less than 5

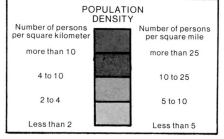

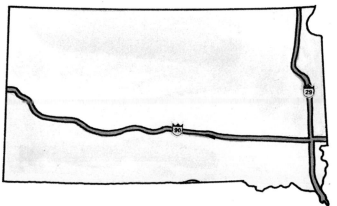

MAJOR HIGHWAYS

TOPOGRAPHY

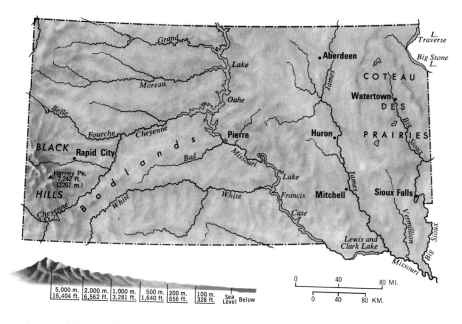

Courtesy of Hammond, Incorporated
Maplewood, New Jersey

COUNTIES

137

Bear Butte in the Black Hills

INDEX

Page numbers that appear in boldface type indicate illustrations

Abdnor, James, 125
Aberdeen, 21, 48, 53, 62, 63, 64, 65, 67, 74-75, 85, 89, 110, 114, 116, 124
Abourezk, James, 125, **125**
Adams Memorial Museum, 116
Agricultural Heritage Museum, 91, 116, **116**
American Fur Company, 33-34
American Horse, **39**, 44
American Indian Cultural Center, 88
American Indian Movement (AIM), 58, 124
Ammons, Edith, 125
Anderson, George Lee (Sparky), 125, **125**
animals, 13, 18-19, **19**, 27, **29**, 30, 101, 113
    state, **108**, 109

area, 10, 111
Arikara Indians, 28-29, 30, 33, 120, 121
Armstrong, Moses K., 74
art, **29**, 34, 78-82, **78**, **79**, **80**, **81**
Audubon, John, 34, 78
Augustana College, 65, 83, 114
Badlands, 7, 12-13, **12**, **13**, 52, 96, 98, 111, 113
Badlands National Park, **2-3**, **8-9**, **85**, 97, 98-99, 111, 118, 123
Bad River, 15, 34, 112
Bannister, Floyd Franklin, 125
Baum, L. Frank, 75, 93, 125, **125**
Beadle, William, 125
Bear Butte, 84, 105, **138**
Beckwith House, 93
Belle Fourche, 65, 69, 70, 83, 103, 105

Belle Fourche River, 15
Big Bend Dam, 95, 112
Big Foot, Chief, 52
Big Sioux River, 15, 21, 27-28, 33, 38, 40, 49, 92, 112, 121
Big Stone Lake, 11, 15, 28, 38, 88, 111, 112
birds, 18, **19**, 85, 88, 113
    state, **108**, 109
Black Hills, 7, 10, 14-15, 16-17, 18, 22, 27, 29, 30, 31, 35, 43-46, 47, 51, 58-59, **64**, 65, 67, 68-69, 75, 81, **98**, 99-105, **100**, **101**, **103**, **109**, 113, 117, 119, 122, 123, **138**
Black Hills National Forest, **14**, 19, 57-58, **58**, 84, 100-101, 111, 117
Black Hills Passion Play, 77, 105, 117

Black Hills Playhouse, 77, 102, 117

Black Hills Roundup, 83, 105

Black Hills State University, 64, 105, 114

Black Hills Symphony Orchestra, 77, 117

Bodmer, Karl, 34, 78

Booth Historic Fish Hatchery, 118

Borglum, Gutzon, **50**, 81, 93, 102, **103**, 125, **125**

Borglum, Lincoln, 81, 125

Brokaw, Tom, 51, 126, **126**

Brookings, 21, 48, 64, 67, 79, 83, 91, 110, 114, 116

Buechel Memorial Lakota Museum, 97

Buffalo Gap National Grassland, 14, 99, 111

Bullock, Seth, 118, 126

Bureau of Indian Affairs, 59, 63-64

Burke, Charles Henry, 126

business, 115

Calamity Jane, 104, 118, 126, **126**

Call of the Wild Museum, 116

Canyon Lake Dam, 57, 124

capitol, state, **60**, 119

Capitol Lake, 94-95

Case, Francis Higbee, 126

Castle Rock, 10, 105-106, 119

Catlin, George, 34, 78
paintings by, **29**, **79**

Centennial State Fair, 59

Centennial Trail, 84

Chamberlain, 34, 48, 53, 63, 95, 107, 116

Chapel in the Hills, **24**, 100, 118

Cheyenne, 105

Cheyenne River, 12, 15, 28, 57, 112

Cheyenne River Indian Reservation, 51, 94

Chinese Tunnel Tour, 104

Chippewa Indians, 29-30

Chouteau, Pierre, Jr., 34, 35, 126

Clark, Charles ''Badger,'' 76, 126

Clark, William, 33, 94, 121

Clement, Amanda, 126

climate, 7, 16-17, **17**, 43, 57, **112**, 113, **136**

Collins, David Scott, 126, **126**

Columbia Fur Company, 34

communication, 71, 115

constitution, 49, 61, 62

Corn Palace, 80, 83, **86-87**, 93, 118

courts, 62, 114

Coyote Student Center, 91

Crazy Horse, 44-45, 102, 126

Crazy Horse Memorial, 80-81, **81**, 118, 124

Crow Creek Indian Reservation, 28, 79, 95

Cultural Heritage Center, 94-95

culture, 74-84, 115-117

Custer, 22, 44, 45, 46, 63, 77, 83, 102, 117, 118

Custer, George, 13, 44, 122, 126, **126**

Custer National Forest, 19, 106, 107, 111

Custer State Park, 18, 77, 84, 102, 117

Dacotah Prairie Museum, 89, 116

Dakota, Indians. *See* Sioux Indians

Dakota State University, 64, 91, 114

Dakota Territorial Museum, **95**, 96, 117

Dakota Territory, 39, 43, 44, 49, 74, 121, 122

Dakota Wesleyan University, 65, 114

Daschle, Thomas A., 127, **127**

Deadwood, 22, 23, 45, **45**, 46, 83, 84, 103, 104, **104**, 105, 116, 117, 118, 122, **141**

Deer Mountain, 84, 104

Delbridge Museum, 92-93, 116

Deloria, Vine, Jr., 76

De Smet, 48, 75-76, 79, 83, 90, 118

De Smet, Pierre Jean, 34-35

Dinosaur Park, 119

Dissected Till Plains, 11, 112

Drift Prairie, 11, 112

Dunn, Harvey, **72-73**, 79, 93, 116, 127

Earth Resources Observation Systems (EROS) Data Center, 70, 119

East River Country, 10, 11, 15, 21, 43, 51

economy, 56-57, 59, 65

education, 62-65, 114, 122

Elk Point, 33, 59

Ellsworth Air Force Base, 56, 70, 100

European explorers and traders, 31-33

Evans Plunge, 101, 119

fairs and festivals, 82-84, **82**, 117

farming, **5**, **11**, 17, 21, 42-43, 53, 55, 57, 59, 65-66, **66**, 115, 122

Fischer quintuplets, 124

fish, 18-19, 94, 113
state, 110

flag, state, **108**, 109

Flaming Fountain Veterans Memorial, 94-95

Flood Control Act, 123

Floren, Myron, 127

flowers, 19
state, 19, **108**, 109

Foote, Mary Hallock, 127

forest fires, 57-58, **58**

Forster, Terry Jay, 127

Fort Berthold Indian Reservation, 29

Fort Defiance, 95

Fort Hale, 95

Fort Kiowa, 95, 107

Fort Laramie Treaty, 122

Fort Meade, 105, 122

Fort Pierre, 32, 34, 35, **35**, 38, 78, 85, 95, 111, 120, 121

Fort Pierre National Grassland, 14

Fort Randall, 35, 38, 40, 121

Fort Randall Dam, 112, 124

Fort Sisseton, 77, 83

Fort Sisseton State Park, 83, 88-89

Foss, Joseph J., 127, **127**
Framboise, Joseph La, 34, 121
Frémont, John Charles, 127
French and Indian War, 32
Friends of the Middle Border
  Museum of Pioneer Life, 93,
  116
fur trade, 32-35
Gall, 127, **127**
Garland, Hamlin, 74-75, 93, 123,
  127, **127**
Gavings Point Dam, 51, 96, 112
gemstone, stae, 110
geography, 7, 10-19, 111, 119
Ghost Dance movement, 52, 122,
  123
Glacial Lakes region, 88-91, **89**
Glass, Hugh, 107
gold, 15, 39, 43-46, 68, **68**, 104
government, 61-62, 113-114
Grand River, 15, 57, 111, 112
Grand River National
  Grassland, 106
grass, state, 109
Great Depression, 55-56, **55**,
  79-80
Great Lakes of South Dakota, 16,
  57, 93-96, **95**, 112
Great Plains, 12-14, **13**, 112
Great Sioux Reservation, 40, 122
Haire, Robert W., 127
Hansen, Niels Ebbeson, 127
Hare, William Hobart, 128
Harkness, Richard, 128, **128**
Harney, William S., 35
Harney Peak, 15, 102, 111, 119
Hart, Mary, 128
Hickok, Jame, 46, 104, 117, 118,
  122, 128
Hill City, 45, 83, 116
Homestake Mine, 46, **46**, 68, **69**,
  103, 119, 122
Homestead Act (1862), 41-42
homesteaders, 41-42, **42**, **43**,
  47-48, **48**, 53
Hot Springs, 22, 49, 101, 117,
  119
Howe, Oscar, 79, 93, 94, 128, **128**
  exhibitions of, 80, 91, 93, 116

paintings by, **80**
Humphrey, Hubert H., 25, 90,
  117, 124, 128, **128**
Hunkpapa Indians, 23, 44, 94
Huron, 21, 48, 59, 65, 66, 77, 83,
  90, 110, 114, 117, 124
Huron College, 65, 114
Hutteries, 41, 54-55, 83, 123
Indian Reorganization Act, 123
Indian reservations, 93-94
industry, 22, 48-49, 59, 66-67,
  67, 69-70
initiative, 54, 123
insect, state, 109
Iron Mountain, 102
James River, 12, 15, 21, 30, 33,
  40, 49, 112
Janklow, William J., 128, **128**
Jefferon, Thomas, 33, 81, 103,
  118
Jewel Cave National Monument,
  102, 111
Johnson, Lyndon, 25, 124
Johnson, Timothy, 128
Kadoka, 98, 118
Keystone, 75, 102, 103, 118
Klein Museum, 94
Krause, Herbert, 128
La Creek National Wildlife
  Refuge, 18
Ladd, Cheryl, 128
Lake Francis Case, 16, 28, 57, 84,
  95, 112
Lake Kampeska, 91
Lake Mitchell, 93
Lake Norden, 90
Lake Oahe, 16, 57, 83, 84, 94,
  112, 124
Lake Poinsett, 15, 88
lakes, 11, 15-16, 18, 84, 112, 117
Lake Sharpe, 16, 57, 84, 95, 112
Lake Thompson, 15
Lake Traverse, 15, 112
Lane, Rose Wilder, 76, 93, 129
Laramie Treaty, 40
La Salle, René-Robert Cavelier,
  Sieur de, 32, 120
La Vérendrye, Francois, 32, 95,
  120

La Vérendrye, Louis Joseph, 32,
  95, 120
La Vérendrye lead plate, 32, **32**,
  95, 116
Lawrence, Ernest O., 123, 129,
  129
Lead, 22, 45, 68, **69**, 84, 103, 119,
  123
Lee, Warren M. Fine Arts Center,
  91
legislature, 61, 113-114
Lemmon, 53, 106
Lemmon, George E., 106
Lewis, Meriwether, 33, 94, 121
Lewis and Clark Lake, 16, 57, 84,
  96, 112
libraries, 105, 117
Lincoln, Abraham, 81, 103, 118
Lisa, Manuel, 34, 121, 129
literature, 74-77, **76**, 90, 123
Little Bighorn, Battle of, 44
Louisiana Purchase, 33, 121
Lower Brûlé Indian Reservation,
  95
lumbering, 67, **67**
Madison, 64, 91, 114, 118
Mammoth Site, 15, **100**, 101
Mandan Indians, 28, 33
Manfred, Frederick, 129
manufacturing, 66-67, 67, 115
maps of South Dakota,
  counties, **137**
  highways, major, **136**
  political, **135**
  population, **136**
  precipitation, **136**
  principal products, **136**
  topography, **137**
maps of United States,
  political, **133**
  topographica, **133**
Matthews Opera House, 105,
  117
McCall, Jack, 46, 104
McGovern, George S., 25, 124,
  129, **129**
Meadowood Art Fair, 90
Medicine Lake, 15
Mellette, Arthur C., 49, 91, 129

140

Main Street in Deadwood

Mellette House, 91, 117
Mennonites, 41
Mickelson, George T., 124, 129, **129**
Milbank, 68, 88
Mills, William Mervin (Billy), 129, **129**
mineral, state, **108**, 109
mining, 15, 56, 68-69, **68**
Minnelusa Pioneer Museum, 100
Minnesota, 10, 111
Minnesota River, 31, 38
Mission, 96
Mississippi River, 31
Missouri River, 10, 12, 15, 16, **17**, 18, 21, 27, 28, 31, 33, 48, 51, 53, 57, 91, 93, 94, 96, 111-112, 121, 123, 124
Missouri Territory, 121
Mitchell, 21, 48, 65, 67, 80, 83, **86-87**, 93, 110, 114, 116, 118, 123
Mitchell, Alexander, Library, 117
Mobridge, 53, 83, 94
Montana, 10, 39, 111, 121
Montana Territory, 122

Moreau River, 15, 57, 112
motto, state, 109
Mound Builders, 27-28, 120
Mountain Music Show, 77, 117
Mount Marty College, 65, 114
Mount Moriah Cemetery, 104, **104**, 118
Mount Rushmore, **50**, 81, 102, 103, **103**, 111, 118, 123
Mundt, Karl Earl, 129
Murdo, 96
Museum of Geology, 116
museums, 115-116
music, 77
National College, 114
National Cowboy Hall of Fame, 106
national forests and parks, **14**, 18, 19, 57-58, **58**, 84, 100-101, 106, **107**, 111, 117
Native Americans, 22-24, 27-31, **29**, **31**, 38-40, **39**, 43-44, 51-53, 58-59, 63-64, 78, 120-122
natural resources, 115
Nebraska, 10, 31, 35, 111
Neuharth, Allen, 129
newspapers, 71, 115
nicknames, state, 7, 109

No. 10 Saloon, 104, **104**
Norbeck, Peter, 123, 130
Norris, Kathleen, 77
North American Baptist Seminary, 114
North Dakota, 10, 31, 49, 111, 122
Northern Great Plains, 116
Northern State University, 64, 89, 114
Oahe Days, 83-84
O'Brien, Pat, 130
O'Fallon, Benjamin, 121
Oglala Sioux Indians, 23
Oglala Lakota College, 64, 97
Ojibwa Indians, 29
Old Fort Meade Cavalry Museum, 105, 116
Old West Museum, 116
Over, W. H., Museum, 92, 115
Owens, Gary, 130
Pathfinder Atomic Power Plant, 124
people, **4**, **20**, 22-24
performing arts, 77, 102, 105, 117
Petrified Wood Park, 106, **106**
Pettigrew, Richard Franklin, 130

Pettigrew Home and Museum, 93, 116
Philip, Scotty, 130
Pierre, 10, 21, 23, 34, 48, 53, **60**, 83-84, 94, 109, 110, 116, 117, 119, 122, 123
Pine Ridge, 45, 63, 97
Pine Ridge Indian Reservation, 51, 58-59, 77, 97
Pioneer Auto Museum and Antique Town, 96
plants, 13, 14, 19, **19**, 113
politics, 24-25, 54, 123
population, 21-22, 110-111, **136**
Powder River, 39
Prairie Homestead, 98
Prairie Plains, 10-11, **11**, 21
Prairie Village, 91, 118
Prehistoric Indian Village, 93, 118
Presentation College, 65, 89, 114
Pressler, Larry, 130, **130**
products, principal, 115, **136**
Pyle, Gladys, 130, **130**
  historic home, 90
ranching, 14, 17, 46-48, **47**, 53, 55, **64**, 65
Rapid City, 15, 21, 22, 23, 45, 47, 49, 53, 56, 57, 62, 64, 66, 67, 69, 70, 71, 77, 85, 99-100, 110, 113, 114, 115, 116, 117, 118, 119, 123, 124
Rapid Creek, 57
recreation and sports, 57, 84-85, **85**, 94, 96, 101, 104, 117
Red Cloud, 39-40, **39**, 122, 130, **130**
Red Cloud Indian Mission, 63, 97
referendum, 54, 123
Reifel, Ben, 130, **130**
religion, 25, 34-35, 41, 54-55, 63, 123
Riggs, Stephen Return, 35
rivers, 10, 15-16, 18, 111-112
Robbie, Joe, 130
Robinson, Doane, 131
Rockerville, 45, 46, 118
rodeos, 83

Rölvaag, Ole Edvart, 75, 93, 131, **131**
Roosevelt, Franklin D., 25, 55, 123
Roosevelt, Theodore, 81, 103, 118
Rosebud, 64, 83, 96-97, 114
Rosebud Creek, 45
Rosebud Indian Reservation, 51, 77, 96, 97, **97**
Roughlock Falls, **14**
Roy Lake State Park, 88
Rushmore-Borglum Story and Gallery, 102-103
Rushmore Plaza Civic Center, 100
Sacajawea, 94
St. Anthony Catholic Church, 94
St. Joseph's Indian School, 63
St. Louis Fur Company, 121
Sande, Earl, 131, **131**
Schmeckfest, 83
Schultz, Theodore W., 131
Shadeshill Recreation Area, 107
Sherman Park, 92-93
Shrine to Music Museum, **90**, 91-92, 116
silver, 15
Sinking Gardens, 103-104
Sinte Gleska College, 64, 97, 114
Sioux City, 40
Sioux Empire Youth Symphony, 77, 117
Sioux Falls, 15, 21, **22**, 23, 38, 39, 49, 62, 63, 65, 66, 67, 70, 71, 75, 77, **82**, 83, 84, 91, 92-93, **92**, 110, 113, 114, 115, 116, 117, 121, 123, 124
Sioux Falls Air Force Training Base, 56
Sioux Falls College, 65, 114
Sioux Falls Stockyards, 65
Sioux Indian Museum and Craft Center, 100, 116
Sioux Indians, 7, 14, 22-23, 25, **26**, 29-31, **31**, 33, 35, 38, 39-40, 43-45, 51-53, 58-59, 63, 64, 74, 78, 89, 94, 96, 97, 105, 120, 121, 122, 123

Sioux War, 44-45, 116, 122
Sisseton, 22, 89, 120
Sisseton Indians, 23
Sitting Bull, 44, 45, 52, 94, 131, **131**
Sitting Bull Stampede, 83
Sleeping Bear Mountain, 105
Slim Buttes, 44
Smith, Preacher, 104, 118, 131
Snow Queen Festival, 82
sod houses, **36-37**, 42, **42**, 43
song, state, 110
South Dakota Air and Space Museum, 100
South Dakota and Open Fiddling Contest, 77, 117
South Dakota Cultural Heritage Center, 116
South Dakota Historical Society, 116
South Dakota Memorial Art Center, 79, 91, 116
South Dakota School of Mines and Technology, 64, 71, 100, 114, 116
South Dakota State Fair, 124
South Dakota State University, 64, 79, 91, 114, 116, 117
South Dakota Symphony Orchestra, 77, 117
Spaulding, Johnny, 105
Spearfish, 22, 45, 64, 77, 83, 103, 105, 114, 118
Spearfish Canyon, 105
Spotted Tail, 44
Standing Rock Indian Reservation, 51, 52, 94
statehood, 49, 109
Steep Wind, **79**
Sturgis, 22, 82, 84, 103, 105
Sylvan Lake, 102
Tabor, 83
Tallent, Anne D., 105, 131, **131**
taxes, 62
Terry Peak, 84, 104
Thunderhead Mountain, 81, 102
Thunderhead Underground Falls, 118
Tibbs, Casey, 131

Todd, John B. S., 38, 39
topography, 7, 10-16, **11**, **12**, **13**, **14**, 112-113 **133**, **137**
tourism, 70, **71**, 99, 117-120
Trail of the Spirits, 120
transportation, **6**, 40, 41, **41**, 47-48, **48**, 53, 70-71, 102, 115, 122, 123, **136**
trees, 15, 18, 19, 113
  state, **108**, 109
Trudeau, Jean Baptiste, 32-33, 121
Tubbs, "Poker Alice," 105
unemployment, 24, 59
United Sioux Tribes Development Corporation, 124
University of South Dakota, **63**, 64, 77, 80, 91, 114, 115, 117, 122

Van Brocklin, Norman, 131
Van Doren, Mamie, 132, **132**
Vermillion, 21, 39, 40, 64, 80, 91, 110, 114, 115, 116, 117, 122
Vermillion River, 15, 21, 33, 34-35, 40, 49, 91, 112
Wahpeton, 22
Wakpekute, 22
Wall, 98, 99, 120, **120**, 124
Ward, Joseph, 132
War of 1812, 34
Washington, George, **50**, 81, 103, 118
Watertown, 21, 48, 67, 90-91, 110, 117
Waubay Lake, 15
Webster, 117
West River Country, 10, 15, 17, 21, 51, 53
West River Great Plains, 10

White, Stewart Edward, 75, 132, **132**
White River, 12, 15, 112
Wilder, Laura Ingalls, 75-76, **76**, 90, 132
  Memorial, 83, 118, **119**
Wind Cave National Park, 18, 84, 101, **101**, 111
World War I, 54-55, 123
World War II, 56
Wounded Knee, 52-53, **52**, 58, 97, 118, 123, 124
Wovoka, 52-53, 122
Wyoming, 10, 39, 111, 121
Wyoming Territory, 122
Yankton, 21, 23, 28, 38, 39, 40, 49, 65, 71, 77, 84, 96, 110, 114, 117, 121
Ziolkowski, Korczak, 80-81, **81**, 94, 102, 124, 132

Picture Identifications
Front cover: Mount Rushmore National Memorial
Pages 2-3: Badlands National Park
Page 6: Central South Dakota plains
Pages 8-9: Banded Buttes, Badland National Park
Page 20: Montage of South Dakota residents
Page 26: An early photograph of Sioux Indians
Pages 36-37: A preserved prairie sod house
Page 50: A 1935 photograph showing Gutzon Borglum (at bottom) and two other men scaling the incomplete face of George Washington during the construction of Mount Rushmore
Page 60: The South Dakota State Capitol in Pierre
Pages 72-73: *The Prairie is My Garden,* by South Dakota artist Harvey Dunn
Pages 86-87: The Corn Palace in Mitchell
Page 108: Montage of state symbols, including the state tree (Black Hills spruce), the state flag, the state mineral (rose quartz), the state animal (coyote), the state flower (American pasqueflower), and the state bird (ring-necked pheasant)
Back cover: Sioux Falls

About the Author

Emilie Lepthien earned a BS, MA, and 6th year certificate in school administration at Northwestern University. She taught upper-grade science and social studies and was principal of Wicker Park Elementary School in Chicago for twenty years. She has written and narrated science and social studies broadcasts for the Radio Council of the Chicago Board of Education.

Ms. Lepthien has written many books in the New True Book and Enchantment of the World series, as well as a biography of Corazon Aquino. The National Federation of Press Women awarded her first place for her book *Enchantment of the World: Greenland.*

Picture Acknowledgments

Front cover, © Dave Brown/**Journalism Services;** 2-3, © **Kirkendall/Spring;** 4, © **Paul Horsted;** 5, © **Greg L. Ryan/Sally A. Beyer;** 6, © **Paul Horsted;** 8-9, © Rod Planck/**M.L. Dembinsky, Jr., Photography Assoc.;** 11, Lens Photo/**Third Coast Stock Source;** 12, © **Tom Till;** 13 (left), © Don & Pat Valenti/**Tom Stack & Associates;** 13 (right), © Rod Planck/**M.L. Dembinsky, Jr., Photography Assoc.;** 14, © **Tom Till;** 17, © **Paul Horsted;** 19 (left), © **Mark Kayser;** 19 (right), © Bill Everitt/**Tom Stack & Associates;** 20 (top left), © **Mark Kayser;** 20 (top right, bottom right), © **Paul Horsted;** 20 (bottom left), © **Joan Dunlop;** 22, © Lani/**Photri;** 24, **SuperStock;** 26, **Historical Pictures Service, Chicago;** 29, **Buffalo Bill Historical Center, Cody, WY;** 31, **South Dakota State Historical Society;** 32, **Reinhard Brucker;** 35, **South Dakota State Historical Society;** 36-37, © MacDonald Photography/**Third Coast Stock Source;** 39, **Historical Pictures Service, Chicago;** 41, **South Dakota State Historical Society;** 42, **Library of Congress;** 43, © Raymond G. Barnes/**TSW-Click/Chicago Ltd.;** 45, **The Bettmann Archive;** 46, **South Dakota State Historical Society;** 47, **North Wind Picture Archives;** 48, 50, **Historical Pictures Service, Chicago;** 52, **Courtesy of Museum of the American Indian, Heye Foundation;** 55, **Historical Pictures Service, Chicago;** 58, **Wide World Photos;** 60, © **Paul Horsted;** 63, © Lani/**Photri;** 64, © **Paul Horsted;** 66 (two photos), **SuperStock;** 67, **Reinhard Brucker;** 68 (left), © **Paul Horsted;** 68 (right), Paul Horsted/**South Dakota Tourist Bureau;** 69, © **Paul Horsted;** 71, © **James P. Rowan;** 72-73, **South Dakota Art Museum Collection, Brookings, South Dakota;** 76, illustration p. 49 from *The Long Winter* **by Laura Ingalls Wilder. Illustrations by Garth Williams. Text** © **1940 by Laura Ingalls Wilder, renewed** © **1968 by Roger L. MacBride. Pictures copyright** © **1953 by Garth Williams, renewed 1981 by Garth Williams. Reprinted by permission of Harper Collins Publishers;** 78 (top left), © **Reinhard Brucker;** 78 (bottom left, right), © **Paul Horsted;** 79, National Museum of American Art, Washington, D.C./**Art Resource, NY;** 80, © **Mrs. Adeheid Howe/University of South Dakota Art Galleries permanent collection;** 81 (left), © **Paul Horsted;** 81 (right), © **Joan Dunlop;** 82, 85, © **Paul Horsted;** 86-87, © **Tom Algire/Tom Stack & Associates;** 89, © **Paul Horsted;** 90, © Paul Horsted/**SD Tourism;** 90 (map), **Len W. Meents;** 92, 95, © **Paul Horsted;** 95 (map), **Len W. Meents;** 97, **SuperStock;** 97 (map), **Len W. Meents;** 98, © Dallas & John Heaton/**Tony Stone Worldwide;** 100, © Paul Horsted/**SD Tourism;** 100 (map), **Len W. Meents;** 101, © **Tom Till;** 103 (left), © James Blank/**Tony Stone Worldwide/Chicago Ltd.;** 103 (right), © Tom Nebbia/**TSW-Click/Chicago Ltd.;** 104 (two photos), © **Joan Dunlop;** 106, © Susan Malis/**Marilyn Gartman Agency;** 107, © **Paul Horsted;** 108 (tree), © Pete Schaefer/**South Dakota State University;** 108 (flag), **Courtesy Flag Research Center, Winchester, Massachusetts 01890;** 108 (coyote), © Stan Osolinski/**M.L. Dembinsky, Jr., Photography Assoc.;** 108 (quartz), © **Paul Horsted;** 108 (pheasant), © Sharon Cummings/**M.L. Dembinsky, Jr., Photography Assoc.;** 108 (flowers), © **Jerry Hennen;** 112, © **Paul Horsted;** 116, **SD Tourism;** 119, © Bill Howe/**Photri;** 120, © **Joan Dunlop;** 125 (Abourezk, Anderson, Borglum), **AP/Wide World Photos;** 125 (Baum), **Historical Pictures Service, Chicago;** 126 (Brokaw, Collins, Custer), **AP/Wide World Photos;** 126 (Calamity Jane), **Historical Pictures Service, Chicago;** 127, (Daschle, Foss, Garland), **AP/Wide World Photos;** 127 (Gall), **North Wind Picture Archives;** 128 (Harkness, Janklow), **AP/Wide World Photos;** 128 (Howe), **University of South Dakota Photo Services;** 128 (Humphrey), **Historical Pictures Service, Chicago;** 129 (Lawrence, McGovern, Mickelson), **AP/Wide World Photos;** 129 (Mills), **UPI/Bettmann;** 130 (Pressler, Reifel), **AP/Wide World Photos;** 130 (Pyle), **South Dakota State Historical Society;** 130 (Red Cloud), **Smithsonian Institution;** 131 (Rölvaag), **St. Olaf College Archives;** 131 (Sande, Sitting Bull), **AP/Wide World Photos;** 131 (Tallent), **South Dakota State Historical Society;** 132 (two photos), **AP/Wide World Photos;** 136 (maps), **Len W. Meents;** 138, © **Ken Norgard;** 141, back cover, © **Paul Horsted**